I0753155

Between Two Skies

From Vietnam Medevac Pilot To Helicopter Cowboy

Other works by John Bradshaw

Elmer Kelton's The Familiar Stranger

written with Steve Kelton

Elmer Kelton's The Blessing

Between Two Skies

From Vietnam Medevac Pilot To Helicopter Cowboy

John Bradshaw

DEVIL'S CLAW PRESS

Paperback ISBN: 979-8-9939675-2-3

To Boone, my son.

Chapter 1

In the spring of 1968, Aubrey Lange was only a few weeks into his first tour in Vietnam, serving as a medevac pilot in the Army's 498th Medical Company, Air Ambulance. At that point, Lange, a Central Texas native who was quick to smile yet small in size, was a copilot, what they called a "peter pilot." He was twenty-four years old but looked much younger.

During his brief time in country, based out of Quy Nhon in Central Vietnam, Lange's Huey helicopter had been fired upon almost every mission he flew and had been shot at so heavily during one extraction that the medevac crew was forced to abandon the landing zone until a gunship cleaned up the enemy troops attempting to shoot them down.

Medevac crews were often referred to as Dustoff, which was their call sign. In late April, two Dustoff crews from the 498th had been sent to reinforce the 571st Medical Detachment, based out of Phu Bai. "This was way up north, close to the DMZ, in what we called 'mean Indian country,'" Lange said. "It was hot. Everything was hot."

On April 29, 1968, three Dustoff crews out of Phu Bai were sent to reinforce the 281st Assault Helicopter Company and Marine Air Group 36, along with other aircraft, in a hot extraction of both American and ARVN troops, in the Thua Thien Province. Those ground troops were taking heavy machine gun and rocket fire from close range. They had suffered casualties and injuries and needed picked up. However, enemy fire was so heavy as to make extraction extremely dangerous.

More than fifteen helicopters flew over on the scene, both gunships and slicks. B-52 bombers and small jets came in with regularity in an effort to clear the enemy positions. Every helicopter took fire and most were hit. Five helicopters were shot down on April 29. One helicopter pilot was shot and killed. His crew was forced to pull him off the controls, and the peter pilot took over.

Three Dustoff crews, Lange among them, were ordered to the site, not knowing how deadly was the fight they were entering. "They sent us in, but we didn't know all that was going on. It was just a mission. Let's go take care of it. If we'd have known all that, we'd have crapped our pants."

Before Lange and the other Dustoff crews arrived, dense clouds moved into the area. The ceilings were too low to fly, forcing a postponement. "We were on the way. I was on the radio, and all of a sudden, we got a call that said, 'Turn back.'"

Looking back, Lange was grateful the mission was

called off that day. The odds were certainly not in their favor. "They were shooting down everything that came in there."

Ground troops received steady enemy fire through the night, the next morning and into the afternoon. They managed to capture an NVA soldier, who revealed during interrogation that an entire NVA battalion was en route to join the fight. Things looked bleak for those on the ground.

Low ceilings still prevented extraction, although two helicopters were on site during the morning of April 30. One, a gunship, was shot down.

The weather broke during the afternoon, and the

extraction was mounted. Jets bombarded the enemy positions, as did artillery from a nearby fire support base called Bastogne. Gunships prowled the area, engaging the NVA positions.

Lange, copiloting Dustoff 60, saw it all. “It was all so we could get in there and get those people. It was sort of humbling.”

The landing zone was in a large valley filled with dense jungle. From the Huey, the jungle below was brilliantly green, and the treetops looked to Lange like they were solid enough a man could walk on them. It seemed pretty to him, even at that moment.

Dustoff 62 was the first helicopter in that afternoon, with Dustoff 60, Lange’s aircraft, to follow. He received a radio call ordering them to land as soon as Dustoff 62 cleared. Just then he watched a jet drop napalm a hundred yards from their position. He could feel the heat.

“I can remember an F100, a little jet, went right by me. I could see the pilot’s head in there as he went by. He dropped napalm, and you could see it like it was happening in slow motion. It went down and lit up a big area off to one side. That jungle was so thick that it sort of dissipated and disappeared.”

Dustoff 62 was quickly loaded, and it cleared the extraction site. The aircraft commander of Dustoff 60 was Chief Warrant Officer Sam DeLoach, one of the best pilots in the 498th, according to Lange. DeLoach piloted the Huey toward an extremely tight landing zone that had been cleared with explosives and chainsaws.

"We went into a fairly tight place. It looked just big enough for us to land."

Eucalyptus trees towered three hundred feet above the jungle floor, and DeLoach set them down in a cleared area just large enough for the Huey. Soldiers hunkered all around when they landed, young men who had been in near-constant combat for over twenty-four straight hours. Many were bleeding, some from multiple wounds.

"I remember this one kid, he was Vietnamese. He was just bleeding like a stuck pig."

The Huey had a console between the two front seats that held a variety of controls and the radio. Behind that was another console that contained the descrambler. The ARVN soldier who was bleeding so severely sat on this console. "He was sitting on that, and the blood was just oozing off him. I had to tell him to move, that he was bleeding on all our stuff."

An American special forces sergeant grabbed Lange by the shoulder and called him "*dai uy,*" which is Vietnamese for captain. He said, "*Dai uy*, go right.

Everyone who goes left's getting shot down."

Including the crew and the passengers, there were twenty-two men aboard the Huey, far exceeding the allowable cargo load. Luckily, most of the men were Vietnamese and weighed less than the Americans.

A large tree directly in front of the chopper forced them to ascend vertically for several hundred feet before gaining any forward momentum. Fortunately, Sam DeLoach was very skilled at the controls. Any excess movement of the controls eats up RPMs, and being overloaded, they had none to spare. "That old kid could do it. He could fly that thing."

Slowly, they ascended through the hole in the jungle. Among his other jobs, the copilot was in charge of watching the aircraft's RPMs, which Lange was doing intently just then. They were in real danger of losing power and falling to the jungle floor below.

The throttle was automatic, but there was also what they simply called a "beep button." The copilot could beep up the engine, which slowly added power. "You couldn't do it with the throttle. You had to do it with that little button. You could slowly beep up that engine."

DeLoach kept steady hands on the controls, conserving all the power he could, and Lange continued to watch their RPMs. "I was watching, and as that engine would go down, I'd beep it up. When we got to the top of that tree, I told him, 'That's all there is.'"

The pilot nosed the Huey over the top of the tree, and they picked up valuable speed. "He just scooted over the top of that tree. When he leveled out, we were really going, because he was pulling a lot of power. I started beeping it back down so it wouldn't overspeed the engine."

Lange believed that later, with more experience, he might have performed as well as DeLoach, but certainly not then, six weeks into his first tour. "I couldn't have done that then. I'd have lost power and fallen back in there. He was a hell of a good pilot."

DeLoach followed the sergeant's instruction and veered to the right, and almost immediately they flew over an enemy gun position. The jungle was so dense that they never saw the gun until they were almost above it. Lange believed it was a .51-caliber machine gun, mounted on wheels, and he was certain the enemy soldiers were attempting to bring it in line with the passing Huey.

"They were just in a little pocket there. The only reason they didn't get us was because they couldn't get that gun pointed straight up."

The NVA soldiers fired at them as the Huey passed, while Stanley Baker, the Dustoff crew chief, unloaded an M16 back at them. Miraculously, the helicopter only took one hit, in a skid.

The entire extraction took just over an hour. Dustoff 60 made one trip. They flew the wounded men to Phu Bai, where they landed just in front of the tower. Ground personnel helped unload the men, although most were still mobile. "We had a lot of wounded, but they were walking wounded."

Later, Lange was told a story by his friend Gerald Miller, the peter pilot in Dustoff 62, the first helicopter that went in that afternoon. Miller told Lange that an American soldier, a lieutenant, was loaded into his aircraft.

The lieutenant was so badly wounded that his companions had tied him to a post using telephone wire so they could carry him. Miller looked back at the soldier, who had red hair and blue eyes. "His eyes were open. Big blue eyes," Miller told Lange.

Miller gave the soldier a thumbs up gesture. Later, Miller told Lange, "I felt so stupid after that, because I realized he was dead."

Chapter 2

Aubrey Kyle Lange was born May 10, 1943, in Brady, Texas, to Marvin and Karlita Lange. "I was kin to everybody in Mason. It was one of those places where if I got in trouble, my mother knew about it before I got home. Those old ladies would say, 'You know what that kid did?'"

Marvin Lange, his father, owned a feed store in Mason, but he was forced to close it during the severe drouth of the 1950s. Many ranchers were forced to sell their livestock, while others spent and borrowed until there was nothing left to buy feed. "People couldn't pay, and he finally had to shut it down."

Childhood was a good time for Lange, in the relative innocence of the '40s and '50s. "I had a great family life. My mother and dad couldn't have been any better." His father was an avid outdoorsman, and he often took his son on adventures. "He was a good dad. He loved to fish and hunt."

Lange and the other neighborhood kids hunted, fished and trapped varmints such as raccoons, ringtail cats and possums. "We'd skin them out and tack them to a wall. We'd get fifty cents for a coon."

Lange always loved sports, but he was never an athlete. He was small and just not as athletic as some of the other kids. “I couldn’t run fast. Couldn’t do anything.”

He had friends from the neighborhood who were excellent athletes. “I’d go play with them, and they taught me how to throw a curveball and stuff like that. So, it was kind of fun.”

He loved to play baseball and could sort of get along with that sport. He also enjoyed football, but he was just too small. “I weighed eighty pounds in the eighth grade, so those big kids pretty well mopped the floor with me.”

His class totaled thirty-nine students, and Lange was the smallest of the boys. “That was good later, once I got in aviation. It’s ideal to be small in helicopters.”

He played trumpet in the high school band there in Mason. He enjoyed it and was talented, good enough to win some awards and tasked with playing solos at concerts and contests. The band director, Martin Hale, was influential in Lange’s life and those of many other students. Hale pushed them hard, almost like a football coach, but he was a kind man. “We’d have band practice, and we might not even practice.” When Hale thought it necessary, he spent the entire practice giving life lessons to his students.

Another influential figure in Lange’s early years was an uncle named Monty Hofmann, who was a bachelor with no children. Hofmann spent much of his time with his nephew, hunting, fishing and working. Hofmann worked at a dairy just outside Mason, and even as a young boy Lange went with his uncle to work at the dairy. "He'd come by and pick me up, and the dairy was just right over the hill."

Young Lange helped gather the milk cows out of the pasture, on foot and usually without shoes. "We were always barefoot at that age."

Later, while in high school, Lange helped deliver milk from the same dairy. At that time milk was still delivered door to door in glass bottles. Lange was picked up at three a.m. in the dairy's small delivery van. "I would carry the milk from the van to the porch."

Oftentimes local customers who were out of town left instructions for Lange to go inside their home and leave the milk in the refrigerator. "I made two bucks every morning, but I can remember buying gas for eleven cents back then."

His dad found him an old 1944 model Jeep. It did not have doors or a top, and for a while it didn't even have a windshield. Lange loved it, though, and used it to get into some teenage mischief.

During his senior year, an underclassman named J.Ann Jordan asked him to the Queen's Coronation, which was done in the Sadie Hawkins style. The girls asked out the boys. Lange joked that all of J.Ann's top choices were taken, so she settled on him. "I was about the tenth choice." Still, the night was a success. Lange was voted a duke of the royal court, and several years later J.Ann became his wife.

Chapter 3

In 1961 Lange graduated high school at Mason and headed for Texas A&M University, which at that time was called Agricultural and Mechanical College of Texas. The name changed to Texas A&M University during Lange's time there. He played trumpet in the Aggie band and was a member of the Corps of Cadets. Hazing was common, perhaps most of all in the band. "We thought we were the meanest corps unit on the campus, and I think we were. We got hazed more than anybody on campus."

The hazing was severe, but Lange was not bothered and even thought it fun. Not everyone saw it that way, though. Some took it so poorly that they immediately dropped out of school and went home. Lange knew of one San Angelo native whose parents dropped him off at College Station, and he beat them home. "He literally beat them home when he found out what it was like."

The band was run like a military unit by a lieutenant colonel who was a powerful man on campus. Band members who made a mistake were called out and berated in front of the others. The lieutenant colonel often made them do push-ups. "We were scared to death of him. He did train on us."

Lange was not a model student, and his grades were occasionally subpar. His grades for the first semester were poor enough that he did not believe the school would allow him to register again. He told this to the band director, who pushed through Lange's registration. "That's how I got through A&M. That school was way out of my league."

He worked his way through college, first at Gibson's Discount Center, a store in College Station. There he sacked merchandise and took inventory. Later he got a job at the Texas A&M Housing Office, working the night shift answering phones and receiving and delivering telegrams. "I did that for several years, even in the summer."

College was fun, but it was not easy. After four years Lange was still short some required classes. "It took me an extra summer and the next fall to get out of that damn place." He graduated from Texas A&M in December of 1965, and he knew he was headed for Vietnam.

Chapter 4

Conflict in Vietnam began in the 1800s, and the Vietnam War as most Americans know it began in the late 1950s. By the time Aubrey Lange graduated Texas A&M, the Vietnam War was rolling. Lange knew he was going, but he wanted to direct his own path, as much as he could anyway. He had hoped to receive a military commission, but those poor grades he had earned in college prevented it.

A professor at Texas A&M advised him to go to join the Medical Service Corps, a branch of the U.S. Army. There, his less-than-stellar GPA wasn't an obstacle, and he could get a direct appointment as a second lieutenant. "Vietnam was booming. So, I got a commission before most of my contemporaries, who were well educated and smart."

A month after graduating college, Lange began active duty as a second lieutenant. He was stationed at Fort Sam Houston, in San Antonio.

Soldiers with direct appointments were not required to complete basic training. All Lange had to do was get a physical and sit for an interview. He always joked about how easy it was then. "At that time, to get in the army and even flight school, all you had to do was turn your head and cough."

The Medical Service Corps was and still is a diverse branch of the army. It included many types of medical staff, from doctors and nurses to medical administration. It also included medevac pilots, which was Lange's ultimate goal. He had always wanted to fly. "I told them I wanted to fly, but that was out of the question, I thought then."

He was first assigned as a personnel officer, after taking a short course in basic medical procedures. Mostly he processed doctors and nurses who came in for their own two-week course.

After some time, he was given the job of recruiting men for the position he wanted for himself—medevac pilot. "I was recruiting these guys. I'd give a speech and tell them if they wanted to fly, this was their chance."

Lange dogged his superior, pestering the man to send him to flight school. After a while, the man relented and agreed to send him. "I just slickered myself into flight school. I wanted to go to gun school, but they wouldn't let me."

It had taken Lange a year, but he had finally achieved his goal. In the spring of 1967, the army sent him to Fort Wolters, in Mineral Wells, Texas, for his first stretch of helicopter flight school. The students were a mixture of medevac, slick and gunship pilots, all preparing for Vietnam.

As a senior second lieutenant, Lange outranked many of his fellow students. He was made the class commander, a responsibility he neither wanted nor enjoyed. He felt the heat from superiors when other students did things he could not actually control. "Guys would be late, and the major would call me in and tell me it was a direct order to get them there. I told him, 'Hell, I'm lucky to even be here. I can't make these kids get here on time.'"

Finally, a captain in a class above Lange's failed out and had to start over, putting him in Lange's class. Being a captain, he became class commander, replacing Lange. "God, I wanted to hug his neck, I was so glad."

He was part of class 6722, known as The Green Hats for, unsurprisingly, the colored hats they wore. The class divided into groups of three, known as "stick buddies," and each group had its own instructor. Lange's group instructor was a large man named Schussler. "Normally there were two to a group, but they were really pumping people through."

Lange and his stick buddies began in a Hiller helicopter. Many students learned in a Hughes TH-55, but Lange's instructor was a heavy man and the Hiller could haul more weight. They usually took a two-hour flight every day, in addition to classroom training.

"They taught us how to stay alive, basically. But they

lost a lot of guys there, from crashing. Just before I got there, they lost some kids when they ran into each other, right over the Holiday Inn. It rained down on top of the hotel."

One of Lange's stick buddies was an excellent pilot. Schussler often complimented both him and the other student. He would tell them how well they had made a turn, or how coordinated they were. "Then he'd get around to me and say, 'Son, if you do that again I'm going to pull your head off.'"

Flight school students were allowed three unsuccessful flights, which they called "busting a ride." Students who busted three rides were kicked out of the class and had to start over, like the captain who replaced Lange as class commander. However, the army needed pilots so badly that the instructors often stretched things, giving the students extra opportunities.

Still, the instructors pushed the students and kept them right at the edge of their capabilities, forcing them to get better.

His first solo flight took place on May 19, 1967.

One student's family lived near the base in a trailer house. On his first solo flight he flew to his house and hovered overhead, waving at his kids below.

"They threw him out of flight school. They weren't going to put up with that, because he put a lot of people in danger. If he'd have done it later, it might have been alright. They'd have had too much invested in him. But they didn't have much invested in him yet."

Lange still has a class photo from flight school. He went down the line, pointing out which students became gunship or medevac pilots. He paused on one young man in the photograph. "Hell, this kid was dead before I even got to Vietnam. Actually, several were already dead before I got there."

After four months at Fort Wolters, the army sent the budding helicopter pilots to Alabama's Fort Rucker, later renamed Fort Novosel, for advanced flight training.

There, the pilots moved up to larger helicopters. The first was a Bell 47G3B-1, which was a light three-seat helicopter with few bells and whistles. "We called them an erector set with a bubble. It had a supercharger, and it would haul three people on a bench seat."

In those Bell helicopters, they learned to fly using instruments. The instrument training was difficult, more so for some students than others. They wore blinders that allowed them to look at the instruments and nothing else.

While wearing the blinders and staring at the instruments, the sun occasionally reflected off the moving rotor blades and gave the pilots what they called “flicker vertigo.”

“It would make you dizzy, and all of a sudden you’d lose track of where you were going. I’ve had it. We all had it. Your brain does something.”

When the pilots got flicker vertigo, they had to remove the blinders and shake it off. Lange nearly busted a ride during instrument training. He was not meshing well with the instructor, and it caused problems. Someone above recognized this and moved Lange to a different instructor, and suddenly it all clicked. “It was completely different. All of a sudden, it was easy.”

From the smaller Bell helicopters, the students graduated to the Bell UH-1 Iroquois, commonly called a Huey, the aircraft they would all soon fly in Vietnam. “That’s where they taught us how to fly the damn things.”

They learned to fly in formation, which was both difficult and dangerous. It was also completely unnecessary for the medevac pilots. Lange never once flew in formation while in Vietnam. “The slick pilots that flew in troops always went in formation, but I never did. It’s a bitch with a helicopter. You’re close; the blades are close. I hated it.”

Lange tried to get the army to send him to gun school, just for the fun of it. “I just wanted to go shoot up some ammunition." The army was not overly concerned with Lange having fun, and he was turned down.

While at Fort Rucker, the pilots-in-training went through a one-night survival school, which was meant to prepare them for the possibility of being shot down and even captured in Vietnam.

Survival school began with the students being fed crudely prepared rattlesnakes and grasshoppers. Lange remembers neither being too bad. "The grasshoppers tasted like stale potato chips."

After dark, the pilots divided into small groups, were given a destination and told to hike there. The instructors served as enemy soldiers attempting to capture them along the way.

"At that time, I think nightscopes were just coming out, and they were playing with them. So, they could see us coming."

Lange and his group of four had a compass, but that was all they had to guide them through the darkness of the Alabama night. Their progress was slowed by brush and thick vines, which they often had to battle for progress. At one point they fell into a water-filled ditch hidden in the dark. It was tough going.

Finally, they came to a road and breathed a small sigh of relief. Almost instantly, though, screaming men ran at them, shouting and cursing aggressively. It was the instructors, and they had been captured.

"At that time, I had a pretty good mouth on me. I must've said something derogatory about the guys that had captured us, and that didn't help me any."

The instructors demanded the pilots get into the back of a waiting truck, but before Lange could climb in voluntarily, one of them grabbed him from behind, by the back of his shirt and his waistband, and threw him into the truck.

The truck roared away, and Lange considered jumping out. But he watched the dark roadway slide by as they gained speed, and he reconsidered. He told his fellow captives to remember that it was training, and their captors could not kill them. "They'd damn sure make you think they were going to, though."

They soon arrived at a makeshift prison camp, and their captors ordered them out of the truck and to strip down to their underwear. Lange remained uncooperative.

"I had this bright idea that I was going to make them carry me everywhere. That didn't work out too well. I was on my knees and they were yelling at me to get up. I told them they could go screw themselves."

The captors were not amused. Two large men carried Lange by the arms to a pit and threw him in. The hole was only a few feet deep but had several inches of water in it. The captors placed a set of stocks around Lange's neck and locked it into place.

The pit was too shallow for him to stand and too deep to kneel. He could support his own weight on his legs, but only if he squatted, which was tiring. He could hang by his neck, which was painful.

"I could feel stuff crawling around my legs and ankles. They probably put some frogs in there. I was hoping it wasn't snakes."

He hung there for approximately forty-five minutes, most of which was agonizing. "I was at the point where I would hang my chin on that thing and give my legs a rest. I went back and forth. I was determined not to wussy out."

He wore a blindfold, but he could still hear commotion and screaming all around. He knew another pilot had been placed in a metal wall locker, and the captors constantly banged on it.

"When they finally got tired of that they took me out. I couldn't stand up."

The men carried him to another location and dropped him. They removed his blindfold and began shining a bright flashlight in his eyes, which was painful. They held something under his nose. It was so severe it burned his nostrils. "It might have been tear gas, but it looked like a cigarette. It had an odor that went right to your sinuses."

They began interrogating him, but he was resolute. He only gave his name, rank and serial number.

After all the captives had been interrogated, they were ordered to dress and then marched to a nearby underground tunnel. The tunnel was small, only just big enough for a man to crawl, and perhaps forty feet long.

The captors ordered all the pilots to crawl through the tunnel, one after the other, in the darkness. Lange hated it. "That was the worst part for me."

It was pitch black in the tunnel, so as they crawled through, all they could do was follow the sounds of the man in front of them. Lange was not claustrophobic, but he was concerned that someone else might be and that they would panic down in that tunnel.

"I was scared they were going to throw some tear gas in there, but they didn't. We finally crawled out of there. I don't know if I could do that now."

Lange and J.Ann were married by then. They lived in a mobile home, and he was dropped off there. When he arrived, J.Ann was not home. The trailer was locked, and he didn't have a key. "I was so damn tired, I finally laid down in the yard and went to sleep."

He had the opportunity to sign up for a survival school

held in Panama, but a man in his unit had been through it and often talked of how rough it was. That class was ten days long and included things like pits filled with defanged snakes that the men were lowered into. "It was that same deal—they can't kill you, but they can damn sure scare you."

When Aubrey Lange graduated flight school, he and all his fellow students were headed to Vietnam. "Everybody was going to Vietnam," Lange said. "Everybody." He took a month's leave, then boarded a flight for Saigon.

J.Ann and Aubrey

Chapter 5

On February 14, 1968, J.Ann Lange drove her husband to the airport in San Antonio. He was twenty-four, she even younger. The goodbye was difficult for both of them. They were young and freshly married. And they both knew not everyone came back. "It was hard to leave her for a year. A year back then felt like a long time."

As Lange was waiting for his flight, he struck up a conversation with a colonel who was himself later headed for Vietnam. That colonel was Dick Scott, who was about to become the commander of the 498th Medical Company, Air Ambulance.

Colonel Scott had already served in Vietnam and had been shot down. During the crash, the Huey he piloted had hung in a tree, and Scott's legs had been burned severely. Still, he was back for another tour.

Colonel Scott evidently liked the young man he met there in the airport because he had Lange moved into his company, the 498th. "That's how I ended up there."

Lange, along with many other soldiers, flew in a commercial airliner to California, then on to Hawaii, Guam and finally Vietnam. It was a long trip, and during the last leg things became very real for the young men. "I know when we were flying from Guam to Vietnam, we could see the B52s coming back from a bomb run, and here we were going in."

Main operations center of 498th Medical Company, Air Ambulance

The airliner flew into Saigon in the dark of night. The Tet Offensive had just begun, and the passengers were told to close their window shades so the large plane could not be seen as easily from the ground. It was a safety measure. "They were shooting at the airliners coming in."

Although it was nighttime when they stepped off the plane, the heat still met the soldiers like a wave. And so did the smell. "It smelled just like a sewer." Lange wondered if he would smell that odor for the next year. It turned out he did not, though only because he soon grew accustomed to it.

Artillery shells boomed all around them, and the new arrivals were quickly rushed to bunkers. "It was funny to come out of the U.S., and all of a sudden you're in the middle of a dadgum war zone. You could hear artillery going off and helicopters shooting."

He was bound for Lane Army Airfield near Quy Nhon, on the coast in the northern part of what was then South Vietnam, but there was no transportation to be had. Everyone was too busy to shuttle a few fresh men.

Other pilots waited with Lange for a ride to Quy Nhon, and they all hung around Saigon for a week or so with little to do. It quickly grew tiresome. "We got tired of sitting around. You had to stay there, because if they called you, you had to go then. They assigned you a bunk, and that's where you lived."

Finally, Lange and the others in his unit caught a C130, a large transport airplane, and flew up to Lane Army Airfield.

When they landed, several members of their unit picked them up in a Huey. The pilot carried a grease gun, a short-barreled machine gun known for its inaccuracy. When they landed, a battle was apparently taking place at the 498th, there inside an American base. Explosions boomed around them, and flares arced across the sky. The crew onboard the Huey excitedly told the new arrivals to jump out and take cover.

Fly by at Lane Army Airfield

"They were just screwing with us. It was fun, because we were all just kids."

Lange was one of five fresh pilots to arrive that day. Years later he learned he was the only one of the five to return home unwounded.

Built in 1965, Lane Army Airfield sat a few miles west of Quy Nhon. Multiple units were stationed there, including several helicopter companies. There were gunships and Chinooks along with the 498th Medical Company, Air Ambulance, which alone had twenty-five Hueys. "We were in a big congregation of helicopters out there."

The fresh pilots were shown statistics concerning the life expectancy of helicopter pilots in Vietnam. It was thirty days, as Lange remembers it. "I didn't know that going in. I knew it was pretty rough, but I didn't know it was that bad."

He is still not certain those numbers were correct, but when he finally arrived, he soon found out that things were in fact rough. "Hell, everybody in the unit had been shot or at least shot at. One guy had been shot in the foot."

The pilots wore helmets, and one of them had recently been shot in the head. The bullet went in the front of the helmet, between the man's face and the interior of the helmet. The round traveled around the inside of the helmet, partially scalping the man.

"We wore what we thought were ballistic helmets, but I don't know. They made us feel good, at least."

For the first several months of that first tour, their helmets were white in color. The bright white was easy to see from the ground, which drew the eyes of those shooting at them and made the pilots' heads a target. Pilots even talked about how they often felt they had to duck bullets that came through the windshield. "Hell, everybody could see you sitting in there."

Soon the white helmets were replaced with new olive drab ones, and Lange felt the color change did help.

"They gave us some different helmets that didn't show up so well."

They carried what were referred to as "blood chits," which were made of silk and perhaps a couple feet square. Lange still has one in his office. "We all carried one." On the top of the chit is an American flag. Below is the same statement written in multiple languages, including Vietnamese.

It reads: "I am a citizen of the United States of America. I do not speak your language. Misfortune forces me to seek your assistance in obtaining food, shelter and protection. Please take me to someone who will provide for my safety and see that I am returned to my people. My government will reward you."

Pilots sat in armored seats, with armor along the back, bottom and up short sides. Armored panels slid into place beside the pilots, inside the doors. "The crew chief or medic, whoever was on that side, it was his job to push that or pull it back."

The armored panels somewhat protected the pilots, although their heads were above them. But the panels also blocked the doors. In emergencies, if the panels remained forward, the pilots were forced to climb between the seats and into the cabin.

During Lange's first tour, he saw many pilots wounded. It happened all the time, it seemed. All their armor helped, but nothing was foolproof.

Medevac helicopters did not carry mounted machine guns and in fact were not allowed to, not with a fully displayed red cross on the aircraft.

"Our theory was, and it was probably true, that our people weren't that well trained in shooting. We'd have got somebody else killed. Our job was to get in there and get those people out."

Dustoff crews were still armed, though. When they flew in the northern areas of South Vietnam, where things were often so hot, they strapped an M60, a 7.62x51 millimeter belt-fed machine gun, under the seat. These were for dire emergencies, such as when a helicopter was shot down.

Pilots and crew members carried other guns, as well. Crew chiefs usually had an M16 in the cabin, and the pilot and copilot were always armed.

For a while Lange carried a Thompson submachine gun with him on every mission, but he soon realized it was just too heavy to justify. "So, the thrill went out of that."

He began carrying a shotgun, but he could not carry enough shells to comfort him. He switched to an officer-model AR15, which was shorter than the standard M16. "We could hang them on the seat, and you could carry several clips. They were handy guns."

He also carried a pistol, a .38 revolver, in addition to a long gun, although he was aware of the revolver's limitations. "About the only thing it was good for was to shoot yourself."

Television often portrays wounded soldiers being carried to medevac helicopters in litters. According to Lange, while they did use litters occasionally for back injuries or certain situations where it was absolutely necessary, litters were actually uncommon. Most of the wounded men either walked or were carried by hand into the aircraft. "They were literally thrown in there."

This was because helicopters were so vulnerable while sitting on the ground, almost like sitting ducks. Time was of the essence. Soldiers became wounded in hot areas, and the enemy troops who had wounded them were usually still nearby. Dustoff crews hurried as much as possible while on the ground so they could quickly get airborne again. "We figured eleven seconds was all we needed to stay on the ground. We didn't want to stay longer than eleven seconds, or you'd start drawing a crowd."

Communication with family back in the States was mostly limited to letters. Lange and J.Ann wrote to each other often. Soldiers could occasionally make phone calls home, but those opportunities were sporadic and difficult.

Back in Texas, J.Ann had lacked fifty-nine hours to graduate college when Lange left for Vietnam. Before his tour began, she had enrolled in courses at Sam Houston State University, but she wanted to remain with her husband until he left for Vietnam. Classes began in January, but he was not set to leave for a month.

A plan formed, and J.Ann's twin sister posed as her at college. She lived in the dorm at Sam Houston, attended classes and called J.Ann in San Antonio with the homework assignments. The arrangement lasted until Lange left for Vietnam; then J.Ann attended school herself. She received a biology degree from Sam Houston State and later taught school in San Antonio.

Lange and medic Anthony following a mission

At Quy Nhon, specifically at Lane Army Airfield, Lange was given a short break-in period then assigned as copilot to a warrant officer named LeFevre, who would serve as the pilot. Lange was what they called a "peter pilot." The aircraft commander flew the chopper, while the peter pilot ran the radio and some of the controls.

Peter pilots also served as backup for the aircraft commanders. In cases where the pilot was shot, the peter pilot then took the controls. It was customary for the aircraft commander to fly the first half of the mission and then turn over the controls on the way back to base, so the peter pilot could gain experience.

LeFevre, Lange and the crew flew to Landing Zone English, which was about fifty miles northwest of Quy Nhon. Various army divisions and battalions were stationed at English throughout the war. There was a small medical aid station with one doctor, and the 498th rotated out Dustoff crews there.

"English was a busy place. That's where we did a lot of good, crazy flying out of. That's where the action was. We'd go back to Quy Nhon and recoup, then they'd send us somewhere else."

Flying to LZ English with wounded patient

They slept in tents at Landing Zone English, the same as at the other smaller sites. There was an ARVN artillery unit at English, which fired 105-millimeter

Howitzers. The guns were so powerful that Lange could feel them from his tent. “It was so loud. Every time one of those guns went off, it would just lift you out of your bed.”

On one of Lange’s first missions, still as a peter pilot, they flew into a village along the coast. Normally, through communication with soldiers on the ground, they knew if the situation would be hot. On this mission there was no such warning.

“We landed, and the ground was just churning with bullets. They were shooting at us across this canal. All of a sudden, the pilot’s window just exploded.”

Lange looked out and saw everyone lying on the ground, trying not to be hit by the incoming gunfire. “I told that warrant officer, ‘We better get out of here.’ Boy, he pulled power and we just shot out of there.”

They called and asked for assistance from a nearby gunship. “They came over and annihilated that village. After that, we could get out and take a smoke, do whatever we wanted.”

Back at the 498th, they learned that the window had not been shot out, as they thought. Instead, a round had hit the rotor head, and a piece of it had come through the window. “Having not been there very long, I thought, ‘Damn, this has already started. I’m going to get blown away on the first day.’”

"That was baptism by fire. I thought, 'My gosh, I have fifty more weeks of this.'"

That was the first of many occasions when Lange would watch the gunships come in to protect the Dustoff crews. Those gun units were very effective, and too often completely necessary. "That's all they did every day, was shoot people. They got where they were damn good. They just couldn't carry enough ammunition."

Later, when the pilots got together over a beer, LeFevre, the pilot, told the story of the engagement. He told everyone listening, "I looked over at this damn lieutenant, and he was grinning and saying, 'We better get out of here.'"

Lange knew he had been smiling, because he often did, but in that moment it was more a nervous grin than one of enjoyment. Still, LeFevre's story drew laughs from the other pilots, so he began retelling it every time they had a beer.

"That warrant officer loved to tell that. There's no telling how many times he told that when we were drinking beer."

Soon everyone began referring to Lange as Smiley, or Lieutenant Smiley and then later Captain Smiley.

"Even when I went to a reunion at Branson, they all called me Smiley."

Missions were common, and on busy days they flew multiple flights, sometimes almost constantly. Some were almost routine, in comparison with the memorable ones, at least. A memorable mission occurred when Lange was still fresh and serving as peter pilot.

Gunship near Dong Ha

They flew out of An Khe in the total darkness of a Vietnam night. Their patient was a wounded soldier located on the side of a burned mountainside. When they arrived and turned on the landing lights, the terrain was too steep to land anywhere nearby.

They decided to hover alongside the mountain, close enough the wounded man could be pulled inside the cabin. While the side of the mountain had been burned, some trees remained, their charred skeletons jutting dangerously from the mountainside.

"The pilot got too close and hit one of those snags with the blade. It took about a foot off the end of the blade."

The Huey began shaking, but the pilot held firm. The

crew members in back reached out the cabin door and grabbed the wounded soldier. It was not overly far to base, perhaps eight or nine miles, but the helicopter was shaking so violently that they were not certain they could make it.

However, the entire area around them was so hot that they did not feel secure landing out there in the dark. "I told them we weren't landing out there. Every night they'd mine that road. They were all over out there. If we'd have hit the ground, they'd have been all over us."

LZ Courage

Both pilots decided to fly the machine until it just would not fly anymore. It was a rough and nerve-wracking flight back to base, but fortunately, they made it. "Damn, it did shake though."

Landing Zone English was set up against the

mountains near An Khe, in Vietnam's Central Highlands. The 498th always kept one Dustoff crew there, and the entire area was also patrolled every night by gunships. The area was constantly hot during Lange's first tour. "We were starting to get into Indian country up there. In '68 that was a really hot area. They lost a lot of people."

A road led west out of An Khe toward the larger town of Pleiku. Every night that road was mined by enemy soldiers, and every day American soldiers ran a mine sweeper down it. "Every once in a while, they'd miss one, and a truck would get blown off the road."

The North Vietnamese and Viet Cong often shot at the U.S. helicopters with rocket propelled grenades, and it was particularly common in that area. "I know one bunch went up there and landed. They got shot at with an RPG. It hit the aircraft but didn't go off. It was crazy."

That same road between Pleiku and An Khe led through the Mang Yang Pass, the site of one of the last battles of the First Indochina War, in 1954. There Viet Minh forces ambushed French forces, killing the majority of them. Lange was told that the French soldiers had been buried standing up, facing France. He was never certain of the story's accuracy, but he saw the graves there. "I don't know, but you could see all the plots on that mountain, where they buried them."

Flying near Pleiku one day, Lange and his team listened over the radio to another Dustoff crew performing a hoist mission nearby.

Hoist missions were the most difficult type of extraction. When the litter was dropped, the aircraft had to hover until it was retracted. "You were anchored there. You couldn't move until you got him out of there."

While in regular extractions the goal was to get loaded and airborne in eleven seconds or less, hoist missions took thirty seconds and up to a minute. "Everybody hated those, because they made you hang it out."

That day near Pleiku, Lange and the crew in his aircraft listened over the radio as their brothers in arms performed their hoist operation. The other Huey was hit, and it went down. "They went down screaming. We just sat there and listened to them screaming, all the way down."

Living conditions for the Dustoff crews were far from luxurious, but they did have it better than many of the other soldiers serving in Vietnam.

At Lane Army Airfield, off-duty Dustoff crews slept in simple buildings roughly made of wood and tin.

Officers had their own rooms, while the enlisted men slept in barracks. When they were on duty, they slept in an alert room so they could move quickly when missions came in.

When the crews rotated out to one of the field sites, such as Landing Zone English, the accommodations were simpler, rougher. "Those old army cots felt nice when you first laid down but were hard as hell after a little while."

One night Lange was asleep in his cot at An Khe when the field site was hit by mortar fire. "It just lifted you out of bed. Everybody rushed to bunkers."

He was lying in his bunk reading at Chu Lai when suddenly he heard the unmistakable sound of an incoming rocket. He believes it was a 122-millimeter rocket, which were commonly used by the NVA and Viet Cong, often with bamboo launchers. The rocket Lange heard coming in at Chu Lai hit a marine barracks only a hundred yards or so from his bunk. "It killed a whole bunch of them over there."

Lane Army Airfield had a large mess hall, and the food was decent, according to Lange. The field sites typically had mess halls, but the food was never as good. "It was a pretty normal, bland meal."

The food was poor enough, in fact, that the Dustoff crews regularly chose to eat C-rations rather than mess hall chow. Later in Lange's first tour, the medevac crews were often able to steal or trade for Long Range Patrol rations, commonly called "lurp," which were freeze-dried and thus lightweight and easier to carry.

They also tasted better than the C-rations. "They were pretty good. All you had to do was boil them. There was rice and spaghetti."

They never drank the local water, and at times clean drinking water was in short supply. Occasionally beer was easier to come by than water. "We had more beer than we had water, and it was Pabst Blue Ribbon. They must've had a shipload of that stuff come in there." Bottled sodas were occasionally available, but it was never a regular treat.

The restrooms were much like those seen in Vietnam movies. They were basically large, multi-hole outhouses with barrels underneath to catch the waste. The smell was awful, all the time. "Kids that got in trouble had to pour diesel in those barrels and burn them. We called them shit burners. If the sergeant in those units had trouble with some kid, that's what they got to do. We had those everywhere at Long Binh, and they sure did make it smell bad."

Mosquitos and other insects were a constant bother. Lange and the other soldiers sprayed themselves with insect repellant, when it was available, at least.

They regularly took malaria tablets, but the medicine made the soldiers so sick that some of them quit taking the big pink pills. "They were hard on you. I'd nearly rather have malaria. They gave you a stomachache and loose bowels. Those malaria tablets were rough. They claimed they would court martial us if we caught malaria, but they didn't."

The Tet Offensive began just before Lange arrived in February of 1968, so things were happening for the Dustoff crews. Typically, they were on duty for six or seven straight days, twenty-four hours a day. They flew often, and when they were not actually on a mission they were still on call, nearby and ready. Missions came in at all hours, because soldiers fought out in the jungles and deltas during those same odd hours.

Busy periods were almost the standard, and during them Lange flew almost constantly. "I can remember flying thirteen hours in one day. That was the most I ever flew. We just flew mission after mission after mission."

Quiet periods came on occasion, particularly after the Tet Offensive ended, but Tet lasted the majority of Lange's first tour.

When a mission came in, the aircraft commander would be briefed on the mission and plot it out on a map, while the rest of the crew went to the helicopter, cranked it and made it ready. "Then I'd run down there, and we'd get in and go. Sometimes it'd be dark as hell."

Quy Nhon

Lange had been promoted to aircraft commander a little over two months into his first tour, so it was he who plotted the mission and flew the aircraft.

GPS would have made things simpler, but there was no such thing in 1968. In the operations shack, missions were plotted on big maps hanging from the walls, using the coordinates that had been called in by soldiers on the ground.

"We didn't have GPS, so everything was done by maps. We knew which direction and how far, basically. Then I had my own map in the aircraft."

The maps the pilots carried were covered in plastic, so they marked the position with a grease pencil. Then they followed landmarks shown on the map. It was rough, but it worked.

“We had it down to little squares, so you could narrow it down pretty close. We got used to it. It’s all we had. But if we’d had GPS, that would’ve been great.”

They had rolling maps, which were supposed to follow the progress of the aircraft, but they were so unreliable that the Dustoff pilots rarely used them.

Nighttime missions were even more difficult, because it was so dark that regular landmarks were difficult to see.

During daylight hours, the pilots followed coordinates and landmarks until they were close to the landing zone. They always had the radio frequency of the specific ground unit that needed a medevac. Once contact was made, the ground troops informed the medevac helicopter if they were receiving fire, and from which direction the aircraft should approach to avoid fire.

Then, the soldiers on the ground would pop smoke. There was red, purple, yellow and white smoke. “But you had to watch the white smoke. Sometimes that was tear gas.”

The rule concerning popping smoke was the soldiers

on the ground popped smoke, and then the helicopter pilot would identify the color, rather than the soldiers calling the color beforehand, over the radio. "If they told us they were popping yellow smoke, there would be yellow smoke popping up everywhere because they [enemy troops] were listening to us."

Lange still remembers the strangeness of it, that they could be roused from sleep, fly out into the jungle darkness of Vietnam, pick up a patient or patients with traumatic wounds, sometimes drawing fire themselves, and when it was over they could lie down and go right back to sleep.

"We'd come back thirty minutes later and go back to sleep," Lange said. "I slept better then than I do now."

Lange spent his entire first tour stationed at Lane Army Airfield, although he was often moved to Landing Zone English or one of the other nearby field sites. After a while he and the other Dustoff pilots knew the areas they worked because they flew them so often.

This was beneficial because they became familiar with the country and with any enemy positions or guns. They knew not to fly over certain hills, for example, because there might be a gun position on the other side.

However, when they were sent to a new area, which happened occasionally, all that went out the window. In those cases, they tried to get soldiers stationed there to show them around. It helped, some. "But you still didn't know everything."

Soldiers survived their wounds in far greater numbers in the Vietnam War than previous wars, partly because of the speed in which they received care. Each Dustoff crew included a medic, and these men were able to give immediate care to the wounded.

Then, the wounded could be to better medical care in minutes. "We could go get a kid and get him on a table in fifteen minutes, the whole trip. That's how good it worked. That's how so many people survived."

Between Saigon and Long Binh

Lange saw countless American soldiers with severe injuries, such as bullet wounds to the chest, who were saved. "Even in the Second World War most of those died, because they couldn't get to them."

(Statistics on this vary greatly, but all seem to agree that the number of wounded versus killed decreased substantially in Vietnam compared with earlier wars. Some of this must be attributed to advances in medicine, but it seems to be undisputed that the survivability of battlefield wounds increased due to the dramatic decrease in time from wound to medical care.)

Wounded soldiers were typically flown to the nearest

medical care, whether that was at one of the field sites or to Lane Army Airfield. Medical facilities and caregivers were very limited at the field sites, such as Landing Zone English.

"They could stabilize him, get the blood stopped, so we could take him to the next hospital where they had an emergency room."

During busy times the Dustoff crews brought in so many patients that field stations became overwhelmed. In those cases, the medevac helicopters would load the stabilized patients and fly them on to a hospital. "That would take the load off the little aid stations. They just had army cots and didn't have enough people to take care of everyone."

Quy Nhon had a surgical hospital with operating rooms. Two hospital ships anchored several miles offshore in the South China Sea—*USS Repose* and *USS Sanctuary*. Both were white ships with the iconic red cross painted on the sides. "They had neurosurgeons there. We'd take all the head injuries there. It was a sad deal. They said most of those we took out there didn't survive those head injuries."

Landing helicopters on ships was common, but waves also occasionally made it difficult. "They'd come up to meet you. I've hit them pretty hard. Everything was pretty tight, too. You had to land exactly where that cross was."

Navy hospital ship Sanctuary

One day Lange flew a load of wounded men to one of the ships, and sailors aboard asked if he could fly into Da Nang and get their mail. They knew it was there but had no way to retrieve it, and it had been over two weeks since they had received any. “They were just begging for it. I felt sorry for them, because they were stuck on that ship. That got old, real fast.”

Lange flew to Da Nang, retrieved several bags of mail, and flew it back to the hospital ship. “They were in tears from wanting that mail so bad. They knew the mail was there, but they couldn’t get it.”

Dustoff missions were rarely routine. They flew into hot areas and landed in tiny openings in the jungle, often so small they intentionally chopped trees with their rotor blades.

The pilots learned what trees they could chop down, and which they had best avoid. They could chop elephant grass. Banana trees were easy. “You could chop them like lettuce. But you didn’t want to get into bamboo. It would tangle you up and suck you down.”

In flight school they learned to make tactical approaches to landing sites. They flew at 1500 feet while en route, because in theory small arms fire would not do much damage at that altitude. “It might nick you, but it wouldn’t hurt you that bad.”

Things got dangerous, though, when the helicopter dropped lower than 1500 feet on approach to the landing zone. If they descended slowly, they made an easy target.

To combat this, they used the tactical approach. Basically, they flew above the landing zone at 1500 feet, turned the helicopter on its side and let it fall straight down. It was a wild ride.

“I got to where I was pretty good at it. We could throw that thing out of trim and let it fall. We would say you could have thrown a brick out the window and beat it to the ground.”

It was a dangerous maneuver, for certain, but the pilots knew tricks to help with it. They kept some power as they fell, and the closer they got to the ground the more power they pulled.

At a hundred to two hundred feet they leveled out, righting the aircraft, and touched down, hopefully gently. "But if something happened, you kept on going."

The Dustoff pilots got so wild with these approaches that after a while the bolts attaching the tail boom to the cabin began bending. "They told us we had to slow that down a little bit or we were going to tear those aircraft up. We were putting too much pressure on the tail because we were falling sideways."

Helicopters pilots of all types—medevac, gunship and slicks—often hung out together in the officer's clubs in Vietnam, telling tales and swapping stories.

They joked about the difference between a war story and a fairy tale. The difference, as they told it, was a fairy tale begins with "Once upon a time." A war story begins with, "You won't believe this, but…"

Most of the helicopter pilots were very confident young men, often even arrogant. Lange said he was the worst of them.

Still, his nickname remained Captain Smiley, because he smiled all the time. "That was a trait. I guess I smiled all the time when I talked."

Different units had their own skills and specialties, and the pilots respected each other's talents. They often talked about it over beers.

The gunship pilots often remarked that they would

watch from above as the Dustoff helicopters landed in tiny clearings down in the jungle, with no room to spare. "They told us, 'Damn, we couldn't do that.'"

At LZ Uplift

"But damn, we didn't want to do what they did."

Lange often had conversations with The Pink Team, an army operation in which a light observation helicopter, commonly referred to as a Loach, was teamed up with a Cobra gunship.

A Loach was a Hughes OH-6 Cayuse, a small and maneuverable helicopter used for scouting and reconnaissance, but also occasionally as bait for the

Cobra that followed above or behind.

Whether they flew this operation during the day or night, the Loach flew low to the ground, inviting fire. They'd burn all their lights at night, making themselves an irresistible target to enemy fire.

"Then they'd have a Cobra or somebody behind them, with their lights off. They'd draw fire, but there was a gunship right behind them."

It was an effective but dangerous game. Many of the Loaches were shot down. Some Loach pilots were shot down multiple times. Lange told those pilots it was suicidal. "They were just waiting for somebody to peck at them. We watched them, the silly bastards. They thought it was a lot of fun."

Most of the pilots, no matter their specialty, thought they were having fun. They were young, and it was all exciting to them. "We had fun with what we were doing."

Lange enjoyed his part. In addition to the excitement, it was rewarding for him to play a role in saving soldiers' lives. "It was rewarding to pull somebody out in the middle of the night. We didn't realize how dangerous it was."

"If you could get that guy, say with sucking chest wounds, where he was shot in the lungs and was spewing out every time he took a breath, with medical back there holding their fingers over his chest, it was very rewarding to get him in there before he died."

The medevac pilots took that very seriously, and they flew their aircraft aggressively because they knew seconds counted. "We'd push that thing as hard as we could to do it. We tried as hard as we could, and it was quite a challenge to do that. Everybody knew we would bust our asses to get it done."

Many of the young pilots, and Lange was certainly one of them, thought nothing could happen to them, despite being constantly shot at and occasionally seeing their friends die. "We thought we were immortal. We didn't think we were going to get hurt. I never was scared."

It was not that Lange or the other Dustoff members were entirely fearless, though. They just placed the lives of those they were sent to retrieve above their own.

"We worried about completing the mission, about not being able to go in there and get someone, or if they lost him before we could get in there. I just didn't worry about getting shot."

His feelings of immortality did fade somewhat later, on his second tour, but they never did on his first.

Perhaps they should have, because soon after being promoted to aircraft commander, Lange had a streak in which he was shot at on almost every mission, enough so that his crew began to wonder about his luck. It became serious enough that Colonel Dick Scott temporarily reassigned him.

LZ English

“My crews were starting to bitch, because it seemed like everywhere I went I got shot at. I wasn’t getting hit. Very few times did I take a round in the aircraft.”

In the daylight they could hear the shots, and at night they could actually see the tracers coming at them. “We’d just cut the lights off and keep on going.”

One day he landed at a firebase and had a narrow escape with friendly fire from a 155-millimeter

Howitzer. “He shot that thing just as I flared to go in front of him. Asshole.”

The final straw for Lange’s crew happened one night near Landing Zone English. They were flying through the darkness, preparing to land and pick up a wounded soldier, when the dark sky was suddenly lit by tracers.

“I think a guy must’ve unloaded an entire AK47 clip full of tracers. It was a wall of tracers, and they were between my windshield and the ends of my blades. How he could miss a helicopter that close, I don’t know. But it was so loud. I could hear those bullets go by, over the helicopter noise, and those engines and transmissions are loud.”

The landing was tight, and Lange chopped down a banana tree as he came in. American soldiers were firing mortar shells toward the enemy. The wounded soldier was quickly loaded, and they were off again.

“After that, my crew thought I needed to go somewhere else.”

Colonel Dick Scott received orders instructing him to send a pilot to Long Binh, just outside Saigon, for ninety days, so that pilot could give a daily briefing to General Neal over the unit’s activities from the previous day.

“They picked me,” Lange said. “I didn’t really want to go.”

But, being a soldier, Lange went, whether he liked it or not. Reports came to Lange mostly by telephone. He gathered the information and presented the relevant portions to the general. “I wasn’t a great briefer. I hated it because I couldn’t fly.”

One memorable report he briefed General Neal on came from his unit. A Dustoff crew was performing a hoist mission when it was shot down in the middle of enemy troops. The pilot and one crew member were able to escape the burning helicopter, although the others were killed.

Enemy troops surrounded the men. There was no chance to hide or sneak away. The only choice was to run, as fast as they could, straight through the enemy troops. Then, in the darkness, they had the misfortune of running directly into an enemy camp. All they could do was keep running, and somehow, miraculously, they made it.

The two men spent the night in the jungle but were picked up the next day. “To live through that, I can see how that could come back and haunt you, just running and running.”

Lange was glad when his ninety days in Long Binh were up, and he flew north again, back to Quy Nhon and all its excitement.

In flight school the pilots in training had been told how dark it would be in Vietnam, but Lange was still unprepared. They all were. Lange was from rural Texas, but even there the nights were bright, compared with Vietnam.

"In Texas, you can fly and there are lights everywhere. Over there, as far as you can see, it's black. You couldn't see anything."

Most of the time they flew with no lights, and they even dimmed their instruments lights. It was so dark that even those dim instrument lights made a glow inside the aircraft that invited fire.

Normally, they were forced to turn on the landing lights on approach, but when the moon was bright, they could land with no lights at all. Lange remembered one night near Chu Lai, which is on the coast. The mission was to pick up wounded men off the beach. The moon was full and the sand was white. Lange landed the Huey on the beach with no lights whatsoever.

One night Lange set his Huey down, without lights, in the center of a circle of tanks. "They had them circled like a bunch of wagons in an old western. There was this sergeant standing down there. I guess he was going to motion me in. I put the front of that aircraft right up against his chest. I didn't see him until the last minute. I told him he could have backed off."

The Dustoff helicopters were often fired upon at night, and they could watch the bullets because of the tracer rounds. After a while the pilots could identify the weapon, to some degree. "You could tell the difference. If it was a .51-caliber, it would be a big red ball coming up. They looked huge. A lot of the small arms you could see the tracers, too."

While hoist missions were dangerous during the daytime, they were even worse at night. Lange only performed one nighttime hoist mission. He was glad there were no others.

Nighttime hoist missions were so dangerous because the helicopter had to remain still for longer than was safe, and they had to turn on the lights to do it.

"When we turned on the lights, hell, the whole world could see you. And you had to stay still; Otherwise, you'd kill the guy coming up."

A Dustoff crew in Lange's unit took fifteen rounds one day, sitting still while hoisting an injured soldier.

One night Lange flew into a mountain range to pick up a Korean soldier who had been shot. "It was about two in the morning and pretty dark."

They were carrying an interpreter, who over the radio identified the Korean troops on the ground.

During the daytime, pilots can easily judge their

airspeed by looking at their surroundings. At night, with no lights, that is not possible, so the copilot read the airspeed to the pilot.

"That's why they have lights on a runway, to give you a feeling, a mental picture. We didn't have that. We couldn't tell how fast we were going."

Lange descended through the dark, guided by flashlights on the ground. When he neared the ground, he flipped on the lights.

"When I turned on the landing lights, there was nothing but rocks. I thought there would be a clear place to land."

They could not remain exposed for long. Lange gave it some quick thought and came up with a plan. "I had to put one skid on a boulder. That's what we did. My crew in the back pulled that kid in, and that was it."

Occasions like that came often, when things were far from perfect but seconds counted. Wounded soldiers were in desperate need of medical attention, and the helicopter could not remain still for long before drawing fire. The pilots learned to make quick decisions, and they learned to make good ones.

Some pilots never made aircraft commander because they could not make decisions fast enough. Some made the correct decisions, but it took them two or three seconds too long to do it. Often that was just too long in tense situations. "That's how people got killed. There was just so much thrown at us all at once."

"We just had seconds to decide what to do. But we were good at it. I thought we were pretty good, to be able to make decisions to get those people out of there."

The 498th often supported South Korean soldiers in Vietnam. The White Horse Division was stationed nearby, so the Dustoff crews often picked up its wounded.

"They were mean sumbitches. It was nice to work for them, though. When you went in to pick one up, you hardly had any trouble because they had already fixed all the trouble out there."

South Korean troops in Vietnam have been accused, and even convicted, of brutality. Lange saw some of it firsthand.

"They were the meanest goddamned people. If they got shot at, they would annihilate the village. They would kill everybody. They'd kill the women and kids, the chickens and the dogs."

The Dustoff crews had significant trouble communicating with the Korean troops, which was necessary for them to find the landing zone. It was particularly difficult at night. “We had a hell of a time.”

They finally got an interpreter, an American soldier named Tom Fagan, who had been raised in Korea and spoke fluent Korean. “That made it so much easier. Before that, we didn’t even know if we were going into the right place.”

In 1968, at an American compound near An Khe, a young soldier stood guard duty when a Vietnamese girl approached him. She successfully tempted him with her body, and the young soldier took her into a bunker for some privacy.

The girl had been sent in as a diversion. While the soldier was occupied with her, an enemy soldier sneaked close and threw a satchel charge inside the bunker.

“It killed her, and it cut his legs off. That old kid was screaming and screaming.”

Lange and his crew flew in, and during radio contact they could hear the young soldier screaming and begging for help. The commander on the ground would not allow them to land until the area was secured, which took a few minutes.

As Lange circled overhead, waiting for them to secure the landing zone, Frank Sinatra’s song, “It Was A Very

Good Year," played over the helicopter's radio.

They were in near-constant radio contact with the ground, and they could hear the young soldier screaming in the background. All the while, Frank Sinatra sang about what a great year it was when he was twenty-one.

"We listened to that song, and we listened to that kid scream. It was eerie. Kind of haunting. Between every verse that kid would scream."

Finally, the area cleared enough for the Dustoff crew to land.

"We went in, and there was blood everywhere. That kid was just screaming. His legs were chopped off right above the knees. Afterward, there was so much blood in that aircraft that we had to hose it out."

Lange later heard the young soldier died of his wounds.

While Lange was never shot down or crashed a helicopter (in the army, at least), he had some close calls. One night he landed to pick up a soldier who had been shot in the abdomen. "His guts were just showing."

As soon as they landed for the extraction, a caution light came on in the Huey. There was an issue with the hydraulics. Lange told his crew they were not staying there because it was too dangerous. He made the call to fly it out of there, hydraulics problem or not.

Ordinarily, they could get a couple good pumps before the hydraulics completely locked up, so he had hope. Lange got the Huey in the air, and he headed for an air force base nearby.

"I told them I was coming in without any hydraulics. By then the controls had pretty well froze up, but they were still where I could fly it."

Before they reached the base, the hydraulics froze up to the point that the copilot had to help him push down on the collective. It took both men to force it down. They landed safely, though just barely. "We just skidded it home."

On another occasion he was at a firebase outside Da

Nang. An orphanage near town was closing, and Dustoff helicopters were tasked with flying the orphans into Da Nang. "We loaded them up, and we had a bunch of little kids."

The *USS New Jersey*, an Iowa class battleship, was just off the coast. Lange had called in to the ship and was told they would not be firing.

Either a miscommunication or a change of plan took place, because the *USS New Jersey* began firing just as they flew past. "I called those assholes and told them I was coming by. It was at night. Just about the time I got there they shot. I could look through that salvo and see that smoking barrel." He radioed the ship and was assured they were safe. Lange did not feel safe in the moment, though. "Can you imagine losing a whole load of kids?"

Lange still has a Democratic Republic of Vietnam (North Vietnam) flag given to him by soldiers at a firebase where they often picked up wounded soldiers.

Many of those old firebases had been built earlier by French troops. They were shaped like stars, with points that stuck out from the center. One of these firebases was regularly overrun by enemy troops, then retaken by Americans, over and over.

"They would get overrun every night. They had a way

to slip out and let them have it."

The invading Vietnamese soldiers would take down the American flag and run up theirs. Every morning the NVA or Viet Cong troops left, and the Americans would take back the firebase.

"I'd go in there and pick up casualties, and they gave me one of those flags. They said they got one every night. It was kind of like a game."

West of Chu Lai the mountains began, and the United States had several firebases built on the peaks. "They had shaved the tops off those mountains. There was artillery all around there. It was ideal, because they could see so much."

Lange took a mission to go into one of those firebases. He was not too familiar with the area, because it was out of their typical range. They were supporting a unit that had lost too many aircraft. On the day Lange went in, the firebase was under mortar fire, and things were tense.

"There was a pad there. They told me not to even hit the ground. We'll throw this guy on there." Lange said okay, not thinking much about it.

As the Huey hovered just above the ground, troops from the firebase threw in the wounded man. Over the radio, Lange was told to hurry up, men in the outpost could hear mortars coming in. “He said they were clicking.”

The Dustoff crew left at full speed, and they were not more than two hundred feet away when the mortars hit. “I looked back and you could see the dust and the smoke. That's how close it was. That bothered me for a long time."

Before they even made it back to base, they received another call to pick up more wounded. "I told them no, we had to get that guy in because he was squirting blood out of his chest."

Over the 366 days Lange spent in Vietnam during his first tour, he witnessed many different types of warfare, some of it up close.

"It was a wild and crazy world for helicopter people. I was glad I was in a helicopter. You could see everything, see every weapon we had."

He also saw most of the weapons and tactics used by the enemy, which was exciting for him. He enjoyed being involved in it all.

"I got to see that country from one end to the other. My first tour was Quy Nhon, about midpoint, and we worked all the way up to the DMZ, way up in the mean Indian country."

Operation Arc Light was the code name used for B-52 bombing runs in South Vietnam. The big B-52s flew out of Guam, hitting strategic targets before returning to base. Lange saw it all in person.

"You could see it in the distance, and feel it. There

would just be a wall of dust from the explosions."

Dustoff pilots were given the coordinates of those runs, and they had to look at their maps and make certain not to fly in those areas.

"I knew guys that got in there, and hell, the damn bombs were coming right by them. It was crazy."

The AC-47 was a twin engine, fixed wing gunship used by the United States in Vietnam. Nicknamed *Puff the Magic Dragon*, they fired three mini-guns and mostly operated at night.

"You could see it at night. It looked like a water hose with those tracers. You could hear them working at night."

Many nights Lange and his buddies sat outside and watched those AC-47s working, seeing those tracers slicing toward the ground.

"We always thought, 'Damn it, somebody's going to get shot and we're going to have to go out in the middle of that and get them.'"

"Sometimes we did, sometimes we didn't."

Lange and his crew were taking fire from the ground during one mission when they were assisted by a Douglas A-1E Skyraider, which is a one-seat, single engine prop bomber used widely for decades by the American military.

The day that Skyraider came to their aid, Lange cheered on the plane's pilot over the radio. "I told him, 'Get 'em. They're about to eat us up.'"

Monkeying around at An Khe

Although the Skyraider flew straight into heavy fire, somehow it was not hit. That surprised Lange, watching it unfold from his Huey. He could not understand how the plane flew into such heavy gunfire and miraculously avoided being struck. "That was ironic to me, sort of strange."

Aubrey Lange left Vietnam on Valentine's Day in 1969, his first tour complete. It was a leap year, so he had to serve an extra day over the typical 365.

There had been times he felt overwhelmed, but he was never exactly scared. "I wasn't scared of nothing at the time. I never hesitated to go in."

Looking back, he sees that it was a miracle he survived. Not all of them did. Some of those that did not were his friends. "Sometimes I look back on it and wonder how I survived, how so many of us survived."

Chapter 6

Aubrey Lange spent his time between tours back in Texas, again stationed at Fort Sam Houston, with the 507th Air Ambulance Company. He was glad to be stationed at Fort Sam, since it was so close to home.

He did not care for the holding unit to which he was assigned, though. There just was nothing to do, and it quickly became old. "It was miserable. God, those were miserable assignments. All we did was hang around."

While some of those assigned to the holding unit were content with the slow pace, Lange was not. He wanted to be doing something. "We didn't do anything. It was a mess. It was a terrible place to be assigned."

About the only high point of the assignment was the several old Hiller helicopters available to them. The machines needed time on them, and only a few of the pilots had much interest in taking joy rides.

Lange and a friend often packed a sack lunch and flew up to Canyon Lake, north of San Antonio. There they landed next to a park and ate their lunch. "We'd eat our sack lunch, then get in and fly back."

He always knew he was going back to Vietnam, but he had no desire to serve another tour. In 1970 he and

J.Ann bought a small ranch, almost three-hundred acres, in Mason County. Their son Kyle was born in May of 1971, only about three months before he was to head back for his second tour. "I *really* didn't want to go back. I dreaded it so much."

Chapter 7

On August 19, 1971, Aubrey Lange began his second tour in Vietnam, this time as commander of both the 82nd and 57th Medical Detachments.

During his first tour his call sign had been Dustoff 11. This time around he was Dustoff 76. The 6 signified the commander of the unit, while the 7 denoted the 57th Med Detachment.

He was stationed this time at Binh Thuy Air Base, which was in far southern Vietnam in the Mekong Delta.

Lange was a captain then, which was the highest rank he would ever achieve. That suited him just fine, though. "Captain is all I ever wanted to be. That's the best rank in the army, to me."

He had always thought it would be nice to be the commander, to be in charge, but in the end he did not particularly enjoy the job. He would have rather just flown missions and left the responsibility to someone else.

Things were slow, mission-wise, and the soldiers under his command had more free time than was good for them. He felt like a referee much of the time.

"Those kids would get drunk constantly. I thought for a while it would be fun to command one. You could just tell people what to do. Well, it doesn't work that way."

By that time, the United States had begun a slow withdrawal from Vietnam. "It was getting kind of lonely over there. Everybody was worried about being the last guy over there and they'd have to turn out the light."

He began the tour commanding the 57th and 82nd Med Detachments, but soon he was ordered to pack up the 82nd. "It went to El Paso. I took the 57th and doubled it up with the 159th Detachment."

The feelings of immortality that stayed with Lange during his first tour faded somewhat during his second tour. He was slightly older, and he had seen more. Things were just different.

"My second tour, I knew what it was like to see a lot of dead folks. And on that tour, the North Vietnamese were so mad at us that if you got shot down, they were going to kill you. They'd run up and shoot you."

The navy had gunships that looked like Hueys but with wider blades. They had .50-caliber guns on one side and miniguns on the other. Those were bigger helicopters, so they hauled more ammunition. They also had loudspeakers. During battles the pilots often played music or blasted sirens. "That supposedly put fear into people."

Lange remembered one mission when one of those navy gunships took fire and went down. "I was ten or fifteen miles away. Before I could get to them, they had already come in there and shot the pilots. They were dead in the aircraft when I got there."

He never even touched down, just hovered near enough to see into the helicopter. "They were dead. We could see that." Lange and his crew called for help, and the navy went in to retrieve the bodies.

"That's how vicious it was. It got kind of dicey there at the end. You had to kind of watch yourself."

He was briefed about North Vietnamese tanks moving south, coming closer to them. "They said they found the North Vietnamese soldiers handcuffed to the controls. They were tied to the controls so they had to stay with it. So, their morale wasn't very good."

Lange's personal goal as unit commander was to make

certain they all did their jobs, but also to get out of Vietnam without losing any of his men. He constantly told his crews to be careful.

On October 13, 1971, two months into his second tour, a Dustoff crew under Lange's command flew out on a nighttime mission to pick up a patient near the Cambodian border. It was raining that night, so the pilots were flying with instruments. Radar contact was lost near the Seven Sisters Mountains, which is a group of seven small mountains rising from the Mekong

Delta.

Something went wrong out there that night in the rain, and the Huey crashed into one of the Seven Sisters Mountains. "They flew into the side of a mountain. All of them were killed."

Ordinarily a Dustoff crew was made of four men—two pilots, a crew chief and a medic. On this flight there were five soldiers onboard.

"Somebody wanted to go for a ride, and then boom. Those were the only mountains we had down there."

According to detailed, handwritten reports taken by Lange at the time, he realized at 2100 hours that one of his aircraft had possibly gone down. Weather conditions prevented an immediate rescue mission, although one was prepared.

Lange's report read: "At 0100 hrs 14 Oct 71, a reasonable time had passed to confirm that one of my aircraft was definitely missing and unable to contact Dustoff Control."

At 0200 hours conditions improved enough for the rescue aircraft to depart, with Lange aboard. They were forced to land as the weather worsened, but by morning the weather cleared enough for them to begin the search.

Lange reported at the time, "I was with the rescue crew

and did not return to the 57th Med Det (HA) until the 4 bodies were brought back to Binh Thuy VN." (One body was not found with the aircraft.)

Downed Dustoff on the jungle floor

In clear conditions and daylight, they were soon able to find the downed Huey, which had crashed on the side of the mountain in terrain too rough for them to land. Lange landed in a nearby clearing, and they hiked to the site.

According to Lange's report, the crash site was on the side of the mountain at 1300 feet, with terrain sloping from 30 degrees to 60 degrees.

The log states: "Jungle, single & double canopy with heavy undergrowth over 98% of the area. Undergrowth consists of weeds and other jungle plants 5ft to 9 ft tall. Area is reported to be moderately booby trapped from past hostile actions."

Four American soldiers rode in the rescue aircraft, including Lange, and they met and were escorted in by approximately twenty-five ARVN troops.

"We had to land way up there in a clearing and everyone trail in there. I went down in there with them. It was thick and hot, very loud. The monkeys and the insects were just screaming at us. That's what I noticed most of all, was that it was so loud."

As they neared the crash site, the Vietnamese warned the Americans to be careful, since the wreck itself might have been booby-trapped already. That gave Lange pause. He had known the area might be mined, but not the wreck itself. "Damn, I didn't know that until then."

The Huey was a burned mess of steel, some of it stuck in the tall trees. "The rotor blades were hanging in the trees, and half the helicopter was hanging. It was all a mess."

Bodies of four out of the five men on the mission were there. The pilots were both in their seats, their bodies badly burned. "That aircraft had burned down on top of them. They looked like burnt marshmallows. Just black."

The rescue party searched for hours for the missing man but never found him. He had been riding in the cabin, and they assumed he had been thrown from the Huey at some point.

They began the difficult task of retrieving the bodies of the four men at the site. The terrain was daunting. The mountainside was very steep, so carrying out the bodies by hand was not an attractive option.

The jungle canopy was too thick to lower a basket from

a helicopter. They occasionally used a jungle penetrator. It was lowered from above, and it was pointed on the bottom to push through the trees. Seats folded out, so men could sit and be hoisted up to the helicopter.

This was considered, but there was no good way to attach the burned bodies to the seats. Instead, Lange flew back to base and retrieved some mesh hammocks.

The bodies were placed in the hammocks. Lange hovered above in a Huey, and his crew lowered the jungle penetrator through the trees. They attached the hammocks to the cable, then carefully lifted the bodies through the jungle.

It was all a sad, distasteful chore. "That stayed with you. The odor. My crew had to touch them, but that's how we got them out. We lifted them out one at a time."

The four men were Ronald Schulz and John Chrin, both pilots, Hugo Gaytan, the medic, and crew member Ricky Pate.

The missing soldier's name was Michael Darrah. He was eighteen years old and the crew chief. Lange knew Darrah personally. The thought of leaving the man's body bothered him, but they could not find him.

Lange felt responsible. Darrah had been under his command. He had also seen the heartache of unknowing, when families never knew if their son was alive or dead.

The U.S. embassy issued a reward; Lange believes it was $400. Lange occasionally visited an officer's club on the base. It was there he had previously met Major McGuffin, who ran the Kit Carson Scouts, which were North Vietnamese mercenaries.

"They were mean, heinously mean. They loved to kill people. They had little knives hanging off their belts. They didn't care what side they were on, but they were good. That major would take them out on ambush missions."

Major McGuffin had once invited Lange to go out with them on an ambush mission. It sounded exciting, but he had a wife and son at home. He also knew his superiors would reprimand him severely if they found out he had gone. Also, the possibility of capture was real, and he had heard too many stories about the treatment of captives. He declined the major's invitation.

Lange told Major McGuffin about the reward money, and the man agreed to send his scouts. "Wasn't even a week went by, and I'll be damned if they didn't find him, way down the mountain."

Lange still cannot understand how the Kit Carson Scouts found the body, in that difficult terrain. "I guess they knew that mountain, though."

The Kit Carson scouts found Michael Darrah's body far down the mountain from the crash site. Lange believes he had been sitting in the open door, probably with his legs dangling out like they often did, when the Huey hit the first tree.

"He probably fell eight or nine hundred feet down the mountain," Lange said. "Those were the only mountains we had down in the delta, and they crashed into them."

Lange flew out to a field site near the Seven Sisters Mountains to pick up the body, which was in a body bag when he arrived. He opened the bag, and he could read the name on the uniform. He remembered that Darrah wore a St. Christopher medal, which is a symbol of protection and guidance. It still hung on the body. "I could remember him wearing that before."

It does not take long for a body to decompose in the jungle, and the soldier had been there for a week or more. "His uniform was still on him, but most of the meat was off his bones. Around his knees there was some gristle. But he had his nametag on him."

The embassy declined to pay the Kit Carson Scouts the reward money. Lange was concerned for his own safety since he had set up the deal. He voiced his concerns to the major who ran the scouts.

"He said, 'Oh, they don't give a shit. Get them a couple cases of beer and it'll be fine.'"

"That's all it cost to get that kid back. At least his family didn't have to wonder. He was a good kid."

One of the pilots had been burned so badly that one of

his legs was missing. The man's mother later sent Lange a letter asking where the rest of her son's body was. She also said, unbelievably, that they opened the casket during the funeral service. The soldier's grandfather looked at his burned grandson and had a heart attack on the spot.

"He died right there," Lange said. "It was a hell of a story."

Losing that crew was tough on Lange, as the unit commander. He had been hoping to get through the tour without anyone getting hurt. "That's all I was there for."

During their downtime, some members of the unit helped out at an orphanage in Saigon. Money was tight at the orphanage, so some of the children lacked essential items. Lange asked his mother back in Texas to send what she could. She spoke with locals in Mason, gathered boxes of donated clothing and toys, and shipped them to Vietnam. The Dustoff soldiers handed out the items to the orphans. Lange took photos and sent them back home, where the folks in Mason could see Vietnamese orphans wearing the things they had sent. "It was kind of fun."

The Dustoff units at Bin Thuy lived next to navy quarters, and they ate with them. The navy ate better than the army, so it was a nice arrangement. "They had ships coming in, and they'd tell them to bring them stuff."

Steaks were common then, and for dessert there was strawberry shortcake. "We ate good then. The rest of the world ate like shit, but we ate good."

Still, the American soldiers missed some of their favorite foods from back home, things they could not get in Vietnam. Among other things, Lange missed milkshakes. One day he happened upon a mobile food stand, a local roach coach that sold milkshakes.

Delighted, Lange happily ordered one. "I took a couple of drinks, and it tasted like a milkshake. Then I looked in it, and there were fly parts all in it. Legs and wings and heads. I got so terribly sick for a while after that."

Dustoff soldiers occasionally ate the local cuisine, including some remarkably large shrimp Lange remembered well some fifty years later. One small establishment had live chickens walking throughout the place. They were underfoot, and occasionally the café's owner would chase them out of the place. "But if you wanted to have a chicken, they went out there and grabbed one and cooked it for you."

They drove into Saigon occasionally, but Lange never felt comfortable there. "It was kind of squirrelly. You didn't know who to trust."

Also, Saigon was dirty, and that never suited Lange. The waterways in and around town were full of black, putrid water. The stench was awful. "It just smelled like a sewer."

While things had been so busy during his first tour, during the second tour too much free time was a constant problem. There just were not enough missions to keep everyone busy and fight the boredom. "The kids wanted to fly, and I wanted to fly."

They played sports to pass the time, but still it was difficult for Lange to keep his soldiers out of trouble. They were too bored, and trouble was too easy to find. "They'd get drunk. God, they'd get drunk. They could get liquor basically free, it was so cheap."

"We all drank a lot. There was nothing else to do. There were officers' clubs, and liquor was cheap. We'd all get together, and after a while we were shit-faced. I was little, and they loved to see me get drunk."

He did not notice much drug use during his first tour in '68. They were too busy then, and too far from a big city.

That changed during his second tour. “People were bored, and one thing leads to another. It didn’t take long for kids to get on it, when they didn’t have anything to do.”

Drugs were readily available from the locals, and they were incredibly cheap. American soldiers took advantage of the opportunity. “They just poisoned us to death."

Marijuana was common, and heroin was a major problem. "You could see the little vials everywhere. It was sad. A lot of them got on it, and a lot of them had trouble. It was a big problem."

Lange only knows of one pilot who got on drugs in Vietnam, and it was a man in his unit. "We sent him down the road. He was a warrant officer."

While the pilots did not give too much trouble, there was plenty with the enlisted men. Medics had access to morphine, and some began using it on themselves recreationally. "They were always getting into it." It became such a problem that they were forced to quit carrying morphine in the Dustoff helicopters.

Free time among the soldiers also led to another distraction—romance. Relationships between American soldiers and local girls were common, both in the short and long term.

Vietnamese women were present on the base at Bin Thuy constantly, either cooking, cleaning or doing laundry. "Those little girls were pretty. They were intermingled with us, seemed like all the time."

A medic in Lange's unit fell in love with one of those Vietnamese girls. Their relationship grew, and he planned to take her home and marry her.

"He was a little old country kid from Tennessee or Kentucky. He was a private, but we were friends."

While it was possible for soldiers to marry or bring home Vietnamese women, the process was lengthy and arduous. The U.S. government discouraged it through red tape.

Supply pickup, Dong Thap province

Often, the soldiers' families also discouraged these marriages, which is what happened with the medic. Lange received a letter from the young soldier's mother asking him to do anything he could to stop the union.

"She said, 'If you can do anything in your power to keep him from bringing that girl home, we'd appreciate it. We're country people, and we just don't understand that.'"

The medic's tour was almost up, so he would not have had time to go through the process before he left. Still, he could have done it from back home, as many soldiers did.

Many American soldiers received drops, which were a reduction in the length of their tours. Lange knew one who got a six-month drop, although he never received one himself.

He was uncomfortable participating in any effort to break up the young soldier and the Vietnamese girl, but the boy's mother had asked him. So, he set up a drop for the medic, sending him home early by about two weeks. Typically, a drop was a wonderful thing, but the medic did not see it that way. He spotted the interference. "Oh, God, he was mad at me. He hated me. He was crying and carrying on. I just stayed away from him after that."

Lange often wondered later what happened with the young medic. He hoped the man's mother did not let Lange take all the heat, but he never knew.

Phu Quoc is an island located off the southwestern coast of Vietnam, in the Gulf of Thailand. Phu Quoc Prison was located on the southern part of the island. It was built in 1949 by French colonists, but during the Vietnam War, the United States and South Vietnam used it to house captured North Vietnamese and Viet Cong soldiers.

Lange and several members of his unit flew there one day to assist with dental work on the prisoners. Many of the prisoners had teeth problems, some severe enough they required extractions.

The prisoners with dental issues all gathered outside, waiting their turn. “They’d squat down out there in the sun.”

Multiple chairs made a line under a small shed for the dental patients. All the facilities were crude, nothing fancy about them. Lange had already been given a tour of the medical facilities.

“They took us in their little operating room, and there was a dirt floor. They said they’d be operating on somebody, and there would be a lady in there sweeping. It was pretty crude.”

They gave him a brief tutorial on pulling teeth and then showed him to his own station. Each patient was given a shot of Novocaine, then the bad tooth or teeth were pulled.

“The first one, I pulled the top off the tooth.” The dentist took over and finished that extraction, then put Lange back to work. “I pulled about fifty teeth. We’d just pull them and throw them on the ground. It was a pretty crude deal.”

When the dental work was complete, Lange was leaning against a post inside the prison. A prisoner approached him, an NVA soldier who in fluent English asked him if he was a doctor. Lange responded that no, he was a medevac pilot.

The conversation was friendly and finally got around to college. Lange told the NVA soldier he had gone to Texas A&M. The soldier replied that he had gone to college at Oxford. "That was eerie. He was a prisoner in there, but he had gone to college in England."

The Mekong Delta was, and still is, covered in rice paddies. The flooded fields in the area produce roughly half of Vietnam's rice. Viet Cong and NVA soldiers often mined these paddies, and they were good at it.

Sometimes Dustoff helicopters were called in after a soldier stepped on one of these mines. They picked up the wounded, or sometimes deceased, soldier or soldiers, but they also picked up the other troops, who when they found themselves in a minefield, stood still and waited for help. "They'd get us in there, and we'd hover around and pick them up. They'd step up on the skids. That's how we'd get them out of there."

One night Lange was on duty as pilot when an unusual mission came in. A .50-caliber machine gun had exploded on a navy gunboat, severely wounding the gunner. The soldier was in dire need of immediate attention, and the boat could not get to shore fast enough. So, the Dustoff crew was sent to retrieve the young man off the boat.

The gunboat was small, so the only way to get the wounded man off was by hoist. Those were difficult enough over land, in the daylight. "I had never taken anyone off a boat at night."

Flying with Lange that night was Richard Slade, an excellent pilot who was invaluable that night. "I couldn't have done it without him."

They sent down a basket, but everything was in motion below them—the boat was drifting and rocking from the waves moving beneath it. Lange could see the whitecaps reflecting in the helicopter's landing lights. It was very difficult to hold the Huey stationary over the boat.

"There was nothing still. If it had been daytime, it would have been different. I could have looked at the horizon or something."

Modern coast guard helicopters have advanced electronics that enable them to hover in place, but not the old Hueys. "We didn't have that. It was all manual."

Soldiers on the boat unhooked the basket and got the wounded man strapped in. Then, as the cable came by again, they hooked it to the basket. "He got the ride from hell before we finally got him in, but we did get him in. That was one of the worst things, but we had to get him in or he was going to bleed to death."

One morning Lange received orders for a mission to deliver a small group of South Vietnamese soldiers whose intent was to locate American POWs. "I took them out to a special forces camp, and then they disappeared. We sat there all day and most of the night, fighting mosquitos."

The South Vietnamese soldiers finally returned, and with a bandaged captive in tow. They did not tell much to Lange, but he could tell they were excited about their prisoner. He never learned what the prisoner might have told them, but Lange does know they did not find any American POWs that day.

During both tours, the Dustoff crews often picked up wounded South Vietnamese soldiers. The tone changed later in the war, when the unhurt South Vietnamese troops wanted out so badly that they would pile into the Huey with the wounded.

"We had a lot of trouble with that. You'd have to nearly beat them back. It was tragic. They wanted to get out of there because they knew they were dead. We'd go for one guy and end up with fifteen."

The North American Rockwell OV-10 Bronco was a

twin-turboprop airplane used by the navy, marine corps and air force. Lange became familiar with them at Can Tho. The navy used them to mark targets. The OV-10s flew low and fast, following the canals and searching for targets.

Some of the Dustoff personnel went out on these missions solely for the experience. Many of them came back nauseated, due to the nature of the missions. Those planes were constantly moving and swaying, following the waterways.

Even experienced helicopter pilots can become airsick when they are not at the controls, which is why Lange declined invitations to ride. "I never did go with them. I didn't want to get sick."

The last time Lange took fire was late in his second tour, in 1972. They had stopped at a refueling station that had formerly been used by the Ninth Infantry Division. Everything was vacant at that point, but there was a fueling station. "It was remote, but we could land and get out."

They were outside the helicopter, walking around, smoking and relieving themselves. They thought they were alone, but without warning a shot came from the tree line and struck the Huey. "It went through the tail. I thought, 'Well, I guess we better leave.' So, we got in and took off."

Lange received many medals and decorations for certain acts over his two tours. He still has them in a case in his office, although he is not overly concerned with medals or awards. Among them are two Vietnamese medals, a bronze star, a Legion of Merit, and twenty-one air medals. "Those were for missions that were a little more than normal."

Lange returned to the United States on August 19, 1972, after 366 days in Vietnam, '72 being another leap year.

He never received a drop, although he wished for one. "I would've given anything to go home six months early, but I stayed the full year, both times. To get a six-month drop, my god. We were so homesick by then."

From time to time he still thinks about Vietnam, and he remembers the violent and traumatic portions. He does not appear bothered by the memories, and he claims he is not.

"I don't dwell on it," he said. "I can see how some of it could bother someone. Especially the guys on the ground firing, with everybody dying around you. That could bother you."

Standby ships in Dong Thap province

Chapter 8

Back in the United States, Lange made the decision to remain in the army. He was assigned to the 507th Air Ambulance Company, stationed back at Fort Sam Houston in San Antonio.

"Fort Sam is a great place. San Antone and all that. It was a great place to be assigned."

Former President Lyndon B. Johnson owned a ranch near the small Hill Country town of Johnson City, north of San Antonio. Several times Lange was assigned to fly a doctor from Brooke Army Medical Center, at Fort Sam, up to LBJ's ranch, so the physician could check on the president.

Lange never met Lyndon B. Johnson on those trips; instead, he mostly hung out with the Secret Service agents while he waited on the doctor to examine the president.

On the flight home from Lange's last trip to LBJ's ranch, in late 1972, the doctor said he had told the president that he would die if he did not quit drinking bourbon and smoking cigars. "Of course, he died just a few weeks later."

For a time, Lange was assigned to a unit called Military Assistance to Safety and Traffic, which they referred to simply as MAST. The unit provided aerial and medical rescue to communities so rural that medical response was typically slow.

The unit flew to accident sites, much like modern privatized air ambulances, which were not common back then. They also transported critical patients from hospitals around the state to larger hospitals in the San Antonio area, including Brooke Army Medical Center.

He flew to many hospitals, some in small towns, others in large cities. A memorable one for its difficulty was Santa Rosa hospital in downtown San Antonio. The helipad was located on the roof, and conditions made landing there difficult. "It was tight, and the wind was so bad."

The 507th Air Ambulance Company began putting together a fixed wing unit called the Health Services Command Flight Detachment, fixed wing detachment. Lange soon found himself in fixed wing school, back at Alabama's Fort Rucker.

He learned in a Cessna 172, then they flew Beechcraft Baron twin engines. He received a pink slip—a failed ride—when the instructor cut the power to one engine just as they were landing. Lange, in a moment of confusion, cut the power to the other engine. The instructor had little patience for that sort of mistake. "He was so mad about that. He chewed on me for a while about it."

Still, Lange progressed as an airplane pilot. He soon learned to fly the Beechcraft King Air.

Upon completion of fixed wing school, he began flying all over the United States, transporting high ranking officers. He flew fixed wing aircraft for two years, until the army disbanded the unit.

Health Services Command Flight Detachment, San Antonio

His plan all along had been to make a career of the army. His family was growing. In July of 1974 their daughter Marsha was born at Brooke Army Medical Center. The army provided security for the family.

The problem was that the only interest Lange had in the medical service branch was aviation. "I didn't want to work in a hospital. I wanted to fly."

He was a captain then, but promotions were difficult to come by in the medical service since there were so many highly educated individuals in the program. It took a medical degree to become a full colonel.

His last station was at Fort Leonard Wood, in central Missouri, where he was the executive officer of a hospital. While stationed there, Lange received a master's degree from Webster's College, in St. Louis.

He did not care for his assignment there at Fort Leonard Wood, and he did not get along with his superior, a colonel. "That was the worst assignment of my life."

The colonel refused to make decisions on anything. This frustrated Lange incredibly, since he had come from aviation, where decisions had to be made immediately and correctly. "That's how he got to be a colonel, because he never made a decision that could get him in trouble."

He had spent eleven years in the army, but he was disenchanted with the military. In February of 1977, Lange resigned from the army and took his family back to Texas.

Chapter 9

Back home in Mason, Lange was quickly hired by the mayor, a local dentist named Willard B. Aubrey. His new position was as grant writer for the city. He had a master's degree in business management, coupled with a decade or so of military experience.

He secured two large government housing grants for the City of Mason, but none of it was enjoyable. He still wanted to fly.

The late Willard Jordan was well known in the livestock marketing industry. He owned Junction Stockyards for a time, and he began Jordan Cattle Auction at both San Saba and Mason. He was also J.Ann Jordan Lange's uncle.

Willard Jordan knew there was a need in Central Texas for an aerial livestock gathering company. Jordan himself occasionally had trouble gathering stock, and he often heard of others with similar troubles. He began pushing Lange in that direction.

"He was having people come in who couldn't gather their cattle. The oilfield was booming, and the cowboys could make three times the money there."

The idea interested Lange. Other helicopter companies gathered livestock in Texas, but not many operated in his area. He still just wanted to fly, and he had found his opportunity.

He began to travel around and talk to those with similar businesses. He queried them but promised not to move into their territory. Most of those helicopter operators were south of him, all the way into South Texas.

He located a helicopter for sale, a Bell 47G3B1. It was the same model of aircraft he had learned instruments in years earlier in the army.

The Bell had belonged to well-known South Texas rancher and politician George Parr, who had run into some legal problems. Lange was able to buy the machine from a helicopter mechanic who had a lien on it.

"I bought it from the maintenance guy. I called the attorney general's office in Austin and asked if they were going to make any claim on the aircraft."

The attorney general's office was making no further claim, so Lange was legally able to buy it from the mechanic. It was too much aircraft for what he was planning, but it was available. "And it had a fresh overhaul."

In January of 1978 Lange Helicopters, Inc. was formed. He began to pick up some business gathering livestock. He had experience handling livestock, both from childhood and later from occasionally working at

Willard Jordan's salebarns. Jordan continued to spread the word. "He promoted me. He was a blessing."

While the livestock gathering business was growing, it was still slow at first. He took a job fighting wildfires on the Mescalero Apache Reservation near Ruidoso, New Mexico, which lasted about two months.

Every day he flew over the mountains of the Mescalero Reservation, carrying two Mescalero Apache firefighters, and in a basket mounted outside the Bell they carried shovels and chainsaws.

They flew around spotting wildfires and fighting the smaller ones. "If it was a small fire, I'd drop them in there and they'd stomp it out. If it was any bigger than that, we'd bring in the bombers out of Alomogordo."

The fire spotting gig took place in mid-to-late summer, when thunderstorms move across the New Mexico mountains most afternoons. Lightning often lit fires, but during Lange's time there were never any serious fires.

"It was interesting, but I didn't make any money," Lange said.

Soon afterward, he got a contract spotting range caterpillars in northern New Mexico, so they could be sprayed with pesticide. "I've told people about this, and they've never heard of it. It's sort of a plague that develops out there periodically."

Lange's job was to carry personnel to remote pastures. They would land, and the state workers searched the area for range caterpillars. When they found caterpillars, they marked the area with flags and called in spray planes.

"I did that for a month and then I got out of there."

Back home, Lange began getting a few more cattle gathering jobs. Aerial predator control took up the slack when things were slow.

King Ranch had cattle turned out near Menard, and one day at lunch Willard Jordan ran into the crew at a local café.

The cowboys from King Ranch told Jordan they had trucks lined up to ship their cattle, but they could not get them in the pen. "They had been trying all day, and they hated that."

Willard Jordan suggested they hire his nephew, which they immediately did.

"I went down there, and these cattle had never even

seen a helicopter, I guess. It didn't take me thirty minutes to get them in a pen."

Word quickly spread, and calls from customers began pouring in. He began working for Bobby Shelton of the King Ranch line and a large-scale rancher. Lange flew for Shelton at ranches near Valentine and Balmorhea. "I worked for him for a while."

The manager was Bubba Whitehead, and he was Lange's main contact with the ranch. On one occasion Shelton's operation was turning out cattle on a leased ranch near Balmorhea. They still needed to check the fences, but it had rained so much that they could not get around them.

Shelton had Lange fly the entire perimeter fence, searching for problems. Then, when the cattle trucks began arriving, it was too muddy for the trucks to get onto the place.

The truck drivers backed up their trailers against the outside fence and jumped the cattle over the wires. Lange was there with his Bell helicopter. "Then I would drive those cattle up toward the headquarters."

Business was picking up, but Lange still advertised. He talked to those in the ranching business, and he left business cards everywhere.

"I went around to banks and left cards. I'd walk the streets and go to banks."

Along about then a San Angelo rancher named Jock March happened to be in a bank talking about losing stock to coyotes. Someone there told him about Lange and gave him one of the cards he had left.

"Jock called me, and he went with me. He had a big double-barrel shotgun." Lange's helicopter was at the airport, and that morning they arrived before the gates were opened. "We just climbed the fence, him with a shotgun."

They killed some coyotes that day, and March was happy with the deal. He told others about the aerial hunt's success. Lange and March remained friends until March passed away in 2006. "He was a good, funny guy."

In sheep and goat country where coyotes threatened livelihoods, ranchers and many other locals loved it when Lange killed coyotes. The ranchers often hauled the coyote carcasses to town so everyone could look. To them shooting a coyote was better than bagging a trophy deer.

That word-of-mouth was good advertising, and it produced even more business. "That's what got me started. When we weren't gathering cattle, we were hunting coyotes."

Not long after Lange started his business, in about 1980 or so, he was hired for a unique job, one he has never done since.

Many South Texas ranchers were having a terrible time with eagles killing lambs and kid goats, and some ranchers had even been caught shooting eagles. Texas Parks and Wildlife received federal permission to capture and relocate eagles, and the agency hired Lange to assist.

They began the first day outside the South Texas town

of Bracketville, in Kinney County. The sky was cloudy and completely overcast, which turned out to be beneficial. “Those eagles wouldn’t go up in those clouds, and that had them pinned down.”

Eagles seemed to be everywhere in the sky. Lange picked one at random and fell in behind it in his Bell, chasing it through the sky. “It started to get tired. You could see its slobber contrailing out its mouth.”

After a while the eagle landed in a tree. Lange hovered nearby, and his Texas Parks and Wildlife passenger scared it out of the tree with a pistol. The eagle flew, and again they chased it.

“The next time he had to land on the ground. I had this kid with me from Parks and Wildlife, and he jumped out and grabbed the damn thing.”

That continued all day. It was easy. They packed the eagles in boxes for transport to a relocation site. The day was a huge success. In total they caught eight or ten eagles. “We caught every one we saw, because it was overcast. Everybody was happy. We were drinking wine.”

The next day dawned with a clear sky, and the eagle-catching game changed. “Those eagles would take me to 10,000 feet. They could do it faster than I could. As soon as I got to them, they would fold their wings and dive.”

Lange would dive after them, but to no avail. When he neared the ground, the eagles just headed for higher altitudes. All day they went up and down, over and over, and they only caught one eagle. "They had us beat. My guy got so sick, after going up and down all day."

They called it quits after two days. The project was a failure, though it made a good story. "We didn't make a dent in it, but we tried."

Bob Farmer, a well-respected Texas rancher, promoted Lange in the West Texas area. One customer, a product of Farmer's promotion, ranched near Orla. The cattle on the place were difficult to move and bad to brush up. One day the owner's son rode with Lange in the Bell.

Anytime a cow brushed up and refused to move, the young man would shoot her with a shotgun loaded with rat shot. It stung the cattle just enough to make them move, and they had to motivate many of them that way. "We were just having to move those cattle with a shotgun."

One cow brushed up in a thicket, and when Lange hovered near, she even tried to fight the helicopter. The young passenger took aim with the shotgun. "I must have had some buckshot in there. When he pulled the trigger, she fell and died right there. He told me, 'Don't tell my daddy I did that.'"

In 1978 Lange began working for Paisano Cattle Company on the Catto-Gage Ranch south of Marathon, in the Chihuahuan Desert of far West Texas. The ranch goes by several names, depending on the teller, but Paisano Cattle Company, the Catto-Gage Ranch and the A.S. Gage Ranch are all the same place, a beautiful, sprawling ranch that comprises right at 200,000 acres.

Back when Lange began flying for Paisano, the late Ike Roberts was foreman and the ranch ran a couple thousand mama cows. Roberts told Lange it normally took twenty cowboys two months to gather the entire ranch, and they usually got about eighty percent of the cattle in the pen. "They had never used a helicopter."

Lange got started that first time, and things went along smoothly. He worked every day, all day, and he got the whole ranch gathered in about two weeks and with about a ninety percent success rate.

Paisano Cattle Company continued to hire him. Back when they ran cows, they gathered three times per year. When calves were on the ground, there were about four thousand head to pen.

Brent Charlesworth later took over as foreman of

Paisono Cattle Company. In 2024, Charlesworth talked about Lange flying the ranch for so many years. “I can’t say enough good things about him. They broke the mold with that guy.”

Paisano had transitioned from mother cows to a yearling operation. Charlesworth remembers one fall when Lange gathered 8000 yearlings for the ranch.

Charlesworth has two daughters, Colee and Emilee, who grew up on the ranch, helping from a young age. Lange was always worried about the little girls when he flew. Charlesworth said, “He always wanted them to wear bright-colored jackets so he would know where they were in the pasture.”

During one gather, Colee Charlesworth had a horse fall on her, with Lange nearby. He saw it happen, but he could not do anything to help, not from the air. The horse fell on top of Colee, and it stayed down on top of her for a time. Lange hovered close, yet not so close as to spook the young girl’s horse, which was still on top of her. He did not know if she was injured, or how badly.

Finally, the horse got to its feet, and Colee rode it up, unhurt. Lange landed nearby and checked on her, much more frightened than the girl.

It had been a terrible feeling for Lange, seeing the wreck happen but being unable to do anything but watch. “He told me later it was one of the most helpless feelings he’d ever had,” Charlesworth said.

During gathers on the Catto-Gage, Lange would spot cattle and get them started toward the pens, then cowboys on the ground took over as Lange flew away to find more cattle. The system worked well, and Charlesworth said it cut both the time and miles on horseback by at least half.

One year, when Paisano Cattle Company had the 06 Ranch leased, Charlesworth asked Lange over the radio if he would like to land and eat lunch. Lange told him, “No, I’m afraid to land because I don’t think this helicopter will start again. I think something just fell off it. I better go to the trailer.”

In 2024 Lange was still flying for Paisano Cattle Company, forty-six years after he began. Over the years he flew the ranch so many times that he knows the country and how best to gather it. “I still know that place like the back of my hand.”

Many years ago, he was flying for Paisano when a horseshoer on a neighboring ranch was kicked in the face by a horse, severely ripping the man’s face.

“His skin was just hanging off there. His whole face was hanging down. We were working cattle over there, and they came driving up and asked if I could fly him to the hospital."

The nearest hospital was in Alpine, many miles away. The Bell could haul three people, so they loaded the injured horseshoer in the middle, with Lange on one side and J.Ann on the other.

The man was injured to the point he had trouble staying conscious, enough that J.Ann had to prop him up to keep him off the Bell's controls. They made it to the hospital in Alpine, although it was a rough trip.

"I was scared he was going to pass out on me. He was turning green. Poor guy." Later, they found out the man recovered and did well.

The Bell 47G3B-1 worked well for Lange starting out, but it had its downfalls. The machine drank roughly fifteen gallons of gas per hour, and it burned oil. It was covered with grease zerks and needed greased often.

The helicopter had a supercharger, so it had a limit of 1500 hours before serious maintenance was required. It was not taking Lange long to put that many hours on it.

"It would only run 1500 hours, and you had to overhaul it."

Any maintenance on that Bell was very expensive, so

much so that Lange had trouble pricing his work because he never knew when a big maintenance bill might pop up. The first overhaul cost thirty thousand, the second eighty thousand.

Shipping cattle in West Texas

A friend recommended that Lange look at Robinson Helicopters. There was a dealer in Seminole, so he drove up to look at them. "And I bought one. They're pretty good, and they're cheap to run."

That first Robinson R22 cost $58,000 in April of 1981. The R22 is a small, light and maneuverable machine. "They were so good for what we were doing—cattle and hunting. They were cheap compared to the others."

He sold the Bell to a rancher who had learned to fly. "They finally hit a power line in South Texas and tore it all up."

Soon Lange was putting a hundred hours per month on his Robinson. The R22 needed servicing every hundred hours, so Lange bought another one.

In the late 1970s, Lange was hired by a man named John Matthews, who had 1600 head of feeder bulls from Mexico turned out on the Kickapoo Ranch, which was 20,000 acres east of San Angelo.

The bulls were of mixed heritage. They were under contract to McDonald's, to be made into hamburgers. The bulls were not excited to leave the pasture, so Matthews and his crew had been having trouble gathering them.

The bulls did respect a helicopter, although Lange ran into trouble when the cowboys tried to help him. The bulls were so used to running through a line of horsemen that they stampeded back past both the horses and the helicopter.

"Fortunately, I could land, and I told him I couldn't do anything when they see you. He knew, and he got his people out of there, and from then on, I could work them. It was funny. They'd just go through them and run off."

That job led to more work for the Matthews family. About 1980, Lange was hired by John Matthews's uncle, Watt Matthews, the well-known cattleman from Albany, who had been having trouble gathering some cattle. Lange and Watt Matthews soon became friends.

"I worked for him for twenty years, until he passed away. Thank goodness I got to meet him. What an interesting man."

Matthews was a fan of flying, and he often rode with Lange while they gathered cattle. He visited the dentist often to have his teeth cleaned, and more than once he asked Lange to fly him to Stamford for his appointment.

"We'd land across the highway from the dentist. He loved the helicopter."

One day Lange was there flying for Watt Matthews while Charlie Daniels was shooting a music video on the ranch. The video shoot was held back into the ranch, far from the highway. When they were done, Lange was asked to fly Daniels to the highway, where his tour bus waited.

"I don't know if he really wanted to go, but he did. He was nice."

Watt Matthews ran some buffalo, and Lange gathered them for him every year. Over the years Lange has gathered other buffalo. They behave differently than cattle. "They're a trick to gather. They're funny. They don't drive straight. You go this way, and then you go that way, all the way to the pen."

Several times Lange worked for Jess Burner, the prominent late cattleman out of El Paso. Burner had turned out Mexican feeder cattle on several big West Texas ranches. "He had locked up about 1000 sections, and he had 21,000 of those calves."

Burner had never used a helicopter, so the calves were

unfamiliar with the machine and easy to gather, despite some of the pastures being forty or fifty sections. Lange could gather 1500 head or more at one time.

The cattle left the Pecos area headed for pastures in other states, and they shipped twenty truckloads every other day.

"I worked for him three times. The last time he had 17,000 head."

Lange gathered goats on many occasions for Tommy and Lellee Hayre near Sheffield. During one goat gather several Mexican herders worked on the ranch. The men wore huaraches and spoke no English.

The goats were scattered across the ranch and would not drive well in front of the helicopter, so they found that the best method was for Lange to haul the herders around and drop them off one at a time when they located a herd of goats. The men, on foot, then drove the goats to the pens. "They had come out of Mexico with those woven sandals, and that's all they had. They knew how to drive those goats on foot though."

The Mexican herders were at first hesitant to ride in the helicopter, but soon they decided it was fun. However, after a couple helicopter rides followed by a long walk back following goats, the thrill wore off for the men.

"About two times of that, and it was all they wanted.

They'd get back to the house with a set of goats and I'd haul them back out again."

In the early 1980s Lange had been hunting coyotes near Tahoka. Coyotes were plentiful there, and he had

been killing about thirty a day. The Four Sixes Ranch heard of it and contacted him to thin its coyotes. It was the start of a business arrangement and friendship that lasted over forty years.

Lange seldom gathered cattle on the Sixes, but he often hunted coyotes from the air. He became friends with the owner, Anne Marion, and she began to hire him to fly her guests on sightseeing and hunting trips.

Some of those guests that Lange flew around were well-known politicians. He flew James A. Baker III, John Connally and the Bush family—George, Barbara, George W., and Laura. All of them rode with Lange in his little R22.

The Secret Service was not at all comfortable with its charges flying around unsupervised in a tiny helicopter. "They nearly died when they found out I was going to fly those people around." George W. Bush spoke to the Secret Service and quickly straightened out things.

"I took Barbara around late in the evening. I fell in behind an old coyote, and she was taking pictures. There was a big old buck, and she was taking pictures of it. She was really having a good time."

One year several of Anne Marion's friends talked her into taking a canoe trip down the Rio Grande in Big Bend. Beforehand, Marion hired Lange to haul his helicopter down there, so he could pick them up and fly them out when they grew tired of canoeing.

The canoe party got in the Rio Grande at La Linda. Lange stayed at a hotel in Sanderson, on call. "The wind was blowing, and when it blows down there a lot of sand comes down into the river."

The women made it one day and one night in those unpleasant conditions, and then they called Lange. "They said it was miserable. I made several trips hauling them out."

In the late 1970s one big Texas ranch had let its horse program get out of hand. Horses had been breeding unchecked for many years, to the point they had eaten themselves out of a home. The ranch remodeled some pens before the aerial gather, and then Lange went to work. This was back when horses were still slaughtered in the United States, so the horses were all bound for Fort Worth. "We started sending truckloads out of there. We never got them all. I don't know what they did with those."

At another point a central New Mexico ranch had a herd of wild horses running on it that they could not gather. "Wild horses are the worst animal for the land. Horses are hard on the land." The ranch bordered an Indian reservation, which Lange believed was the source of the horses.

Studs, mares and colts made up small horse bands on this ranch. A big wire trap sat in the center of the operation, which is where Lange penned the horses.

At first, he tried pushing bands together before heading to the pens, but the studs fought too much. He soon found that the best method was to gather them in their usual bands, rather than try to push the bands together and drive them all. The horses drove better that way.

"You had to take this stud, with this little bunch. I'd put them in that trap, then get another bunch and put them in that trap."

He ended up with about sixty head of horses in the wire trap, but then he had to drive the entire herd several miles to a pen where they could be loaded. Surprisingly, the entire herd drove nicely. "They all strung out. Once they were out of their area, they just got along. We went straight to the pens with them."

A rancher near Mertzon once had emus in a pasture that he wanted rid of, so he hired Lange to gather them. He got it done, but the emus did not drive well and were incredibly slow to gather. "I drove them, just piddling along. They finally went through the gate. I'd hate to do that all the time. Damn, it was slow."

In the early 2000s a bank hired Lange to gather cattle off a ranch near Haskell that the bank had taken over.

The pens were old, dilapidated and small. The cattle herd had not been tended to for years. Some old, branded cows ran with the herd, but the majority were big mavericks that had never been touched, many of them grown bulls. The entire herd totaled sixty or eighty head.

Lange began flying the place, and he was able to drive cattle into the small pens. “I could get them in the pen, but you couldn’t get the gate shut fast enough. They’d just run back out.”

He talked to the bank, and another plan was devised. The bank hired several good cowboys headed up by Billy Lamb of Haskell.

Each of those cowboys brought two or three horses. The salebarn that was to receive the cattle sent a crew pulling a trailer with a winch mounted in the front.

They made another attempt to pen the cattle from the air, but once again most ran back out before the gate could be shut.

So, Lange began driving the cattle into a brushy corner that bordered a field, sort of an old deer plot. He held up the cattle there, and then he let two or three head at a time break free. The cattle ran past the helicopter and into the field, where the cowboys waited.

When the cattle entered the somewhat open field, the cowboys lined them out and roped them. They then tied down the cattle and left them for the salebarn crew, which came around and dragged them into the trailer with the winch.

"They were good. They could slap a rope on them. They'd rope two or three, and then they'd go switch horses. They had some good horses, too."

Waylon Davis, who was just a long teenager then, told of Cody Aaron roping the biggest bull in the herd, an old horned Hereford-cross estimated to weigh two thousand pounds. Aaron lined out the bull down a two-track ranch road. Davis said, “I saw Hollywood (Aaron) run and rope that bull. He waved his slack down that bull’s back and jerked him over backward. It was pretty impressive.”

Chapter 10

Predator hunting helped pay the bills when Lange first got in business, and it was a significant portion of his business for the next forty-five years.

Herman Couch, owner of the Big Canyon Ranch near Sanderson, had been suffering livestock losses for some time. Lange flew the ranch many times and took some coyotes, but the livestock losses continued. Oftentimes when the killing of livestock begins, it is a particular coyote that develops the habit and does most or all the depredations. Neither Lange nor hunters on the ground could find this killer.

Then one day Lange was conducting a deer survey on the ranch with Monty Harkins riding as passenger when they spotted a lone coyote. "Of course, we had the doors on." Normally the gunner's door is removed so he can shoot more easily, but they weren't hunting that day.

They did have a gun, and Harkins was able to stick the rifle out the small window in the helicopter's door. It was not simple, but they were able to shoot that coyote. After that, the livestock depredation stopped. "They said that coyote had cost them twenty grand in losses, trapper fees and helicopter time. When we killed him, it kind of quit."

Coyote numbers increased outside the historic sheep and goat range, where they were hunted with fever for many decades. When Lange flew in areas north and west of San Angelo, he often got into some heavy coyote populations.

The Four Sixes Ranch was like that, even though for years Lange was hired to thin the ranch's coyotes. On one memorable day, they killed one hundred and four coyotes. In ten days on the ranch, they killed close to 1000. "They were everywhere. We'd be after one and jump another. We'd find a dead cow and there'd be ten or twelve on her."

For years Lange and most other aerial hunters only used shotguns. But when feral hogs became so prevalent, most transitioned to AR rifles.

"You just couldn't carry enough ammunition for a shotgun. An AR, after a while, you pick it up and it's easy. It's not as hard on you, either. A 12-gauge will beat you to death after a while."

During his first years in the predator control business, feral hogs were few and far between. "When I first started, there weren't any pigs in the country. I hardly saw one."

As time passed, feral hogs moved into those previously unpopulated areas and eventually became thick. He and his son Kyle once shot ninety wild hogs in one day. "I was tired of shooting pigs. You wouldn't think you'd ever get that way, but I was just tired of shooting pigs."

Paid helicopter hunts became legal and popular late in Lange's career, and many other helicopter companies embraced it. Lange took up some paid hunters after legalization in Texas, but he soon grew tired of dealing with inexperienced gunners. Some were outright dangerous. "If you look at our skids, they've got holes in them."

Gunners were told to always point the gun down so they did not accidentally shoot the rotor blades. This rule proved to be more difficult to follow than it seems it should. "Those blades cost forty grand apiece, or something like that. It's crazy."

While the vast majority of Lange's business was livestock gathering and predator control, over the years he took some jobs that involved neither.

He flew for an alligator farm near Winnie, which is outside Houston. Helicopters are a common tool on alligator farms in Texas and Louisiana.

The farm Lange flew for harvested the alligator eggs from nests, hatched them, and then grew the animals to four feet before they were slaughtered for meat. Lange flew the owner over his leased land, searching for alligator nests.

"He had leased land all over, and he had to go around to all these places and find these nests. He would mark them with GPS and then his kids would go in there on an airboat and take the eggs."

Lange spent much of one spring helping count prairie chickens in the Texas Panhandle, New Mexico,

Oklahoma and Kansas. Wildlife biologists rode with him, counting prairie chickens, day in and day out.

“I did that several years in the spring,” Lange said. “I got tired of that. I flew all over the country counting prairie chickens. We have pilots who enjoy doing this, so they’ve continued it.”

For many years Lange flew for farms in South Texas, Arkansas and eastern Louisiana, pollinating rice fields. A large customer was a rice farmer near Alvin, Texas. The 6000-acre farm grew a variety of hybrid rice that did not self-pollinate, so they brought in helicopters to spread the pollen with the rotor wash.

The farm had alternating rows of hybrid and non-hybrid rice. Fifteen or more helicopters usually worked the place, and they flew back and forth, spreading the pollen. “What we did is fly down that regular rice row and scatter that pollen.”

They flew twenty-five miles per hour, two-and-a-half feet above the top of the plants, row after row, turning around at the end of the field and going back.

The Robinson R22 was the perfect helicopter for the job. Larger helicopters produce too much wind, which damages the rice plant.

Conditions had to be just right for pollination, and those conditions never lasted long, which is why so many helicopters were used. Conditions usually became right at about ten in the morning and lasted about three hours. “We’d do the same field every day for a week or ten days, stirring it up.”

Each day, when conditions became right, the group of small helicopters left out together. Lange was the oldest pilot, so he always led them out. Their morning departures were always orderly, organized and safe.

Their returns were never as neat. Robinson helicopters came in from all directions, racing for the landing zone. “Everybody was coming in from everywhere, because everybody was running out of gas.”

Conditions stayed right for about three hours, which is all a tank of gas will last in an R22. “But by golly you better be on the ground at 2:59.”

It was a good, steady gig for any pilot, but it was also a good training ground for newer pilots. “It was good for kids needing to get time. It was ideal for them.”

Because some of the pilots were inexperienced, and also because the job became boring after a while, there were occasional minor crashes.

“It was amazing the kids that got hurt or tore up stuff. One kid fell asleep and landed in the field.”

They used GPS to stay on track. Lange said this was necessary, because after a while of flying back and forth for hours, they got in a daze and would have lost track of where they were going.

Some of the pilots listened to music to pass the time. One day it was hot, and Lange was just looking for something different to do. So, he was flying along with his head sticking out the door when a bee flew underneath his sunglasses and got stuck.

"I knew it was a bee. I was about halfway across that field, and I whipped that thing around and landed before it stung me. I got it on the ground, lifted those glasses up and flicked him away." He quit sticking his head out the window after that.

The daughter of a wealthy Dallas family got married at Buster Welch's ranch near Rotan. The wedding planner hired Lange to carry around a professional photographer so aerial photos could be taken of the wedding.

When the aerial photos were complete, the wedding planner told Lange they were running out of liquor and asked if he would fly to Sweetwater to the liquor store. “I was in that little Robinson, so I couldn’t carry much but I said sure.”

He found the liquor store in Sweetwater, and there was a vacant lot next to it. Nearby were some low-rent housing and apartments. “When I landed, there were kids jumping out the windows to come see me. I had to shut down fast.”

The wedding planner had called ahead with the order. Lange ran inside the liquor store, trying to hurry before the neighborhood kids tore up his Robinson or flew away in it. The liquor store had recently sold a winning lottery ticket, and there was a long line of lottery hopefuls. Finally, he was able to get the liquor order and go outside.

“They bought several cases of high-end liquor, which was about all I could carry.”

The neighborhood kids still surrounded his helicopter when he came out of the store. Just as he was preparing to crank his Robinson, a local policeman showed up and told him he could not land a helicopter there. “I told him, ‘Don’t worry, I’ll never land here again in my life. I need to get this thing cranked before these kids kill themselves.’”

One year Lange worked for the Rolling Plains Quail Research Ranch at Roby. Some of the quail were outfitted with radio collars, and the researchers occasionally needed to locate them. They mounted antennas on Lange's Cessna 182, then they flew around the ranch listening for the beeps on the transmitters.

When they heard a beep, Lange circled until they zeroed in on the quail's location. After that a crew on the ground took over.

For a while they flew at a low altitude, about five hundred feet, but it got very hot in the Cessna at that altitude. "Everybody got sick as hell, so I got up to about a thousand feet, where it was cooler."

Wildlife capture became a large part of Lange Helicopters, and over the years Lange and his son Kyle have captured many types of animals, including white-tailed deer, axis, fallow, elk, aoudad, Père David's deer, scimitar-horned oryx and more.

Aerial capture requires very aggressive flying, more than any of the other things Lange did in his business. They never captured with a full tank of gas, just to keep the weight down. "You've got to fly it hard. It's hard on the aircraft."

In the beginning, they bought a New Zealand-style netgun and received a week of training on how to capture animals from the air. The net has four weights, one on each corner, that are packed in a canister.

The gun is a bolt action rifle that shoots a .308 blank. "It's loud, and it kicks pretty hard." The nets come in different sizes, for different animals.

The helicopter must fly low, about fifteen feet above the target animal, which is of course running and dodging. It is difficult and dangerous flying.

The ground crew follows closely on ATVs. When the animal is netted, the ground crew quickly jumps on it. "You need somebody to get to that animal as soon as they can."

The ground crew holds down the animal, removes it from the net and ties its legs together. It can then be loaded onto an ATV or into a trailer. It is hard work, particularly with bigger animals. "That's a young man's game, I tell you."

When they first got started, the Kickapoo Ranch, which is 20,000 acres southeast of San Angelo, was covered with blackbuck antelope. The population was out of control.

Kyle Lange got together a big crew, and they began

catching the blackbuck. It was hard work. Blackbuck antelope are one of the fastest land animals. "Blackbuck are hard to catch."

The ranch offered to give the animals to the Langes, just to get rid of them, but in the end, they shared the proceeds from the sale of the captured blackbuck.

They sold the animals live, both to private buyers and at exotic sales. "Kyle did all that. He's the one that's good at that."

Several times they have caught elk, which require more men on the ground crew, due to the size of the elk but also because of their behavior. "They're kicking sumbitches. You have to get a rope on its back legs quick."

Of all the animals Lange captured, zebras were perhaps the most difficult. He captured some of them in South Texas. "They'll bite you so bad. We had to put a hog noose around their nose. And they kick so much, too."

One day Lange was flying near Albany on the Nail Ranch with Kyle manning the netgun. They were catching white-tailed deer. Kyle wore his seatbelt but also a shoulder rig, a safety device since the gunner firing the netgun must lean so far out the door.

As Kyle leaned out to fire the netgun, the seatbelt broke and Kyle fell out of the helicopter. Fortunately, the safety harness caught him. "He was dangling. I saw him roll out, and I could see his shadow out there. I just went over and landed."

Aubrey and Kyle

Lange said he never had time to be scared for his son. It all happened too fast. "Everybody got a big laugh out of it."

He once worked with researchers who were capturing white-tailed deer on the YO Ranch near Kerrville. The researchers had set up a long net, and the plan was for Lange to use his helicopter to drive the deer into it. The ground crew would then manually capture the deer.

The net was new and bright white, and the deer

repeatedly saw it and turned away. "As soon as they saw it, they'd turn around and I couldn't get them any closer."

Lange and the researchers discussed the problem, and the researchers went to town and bought a load of dye. They mixed the dye in a barrel and soaked the net in it. "It came out brown. From then on, those deer wouldn't even stop. They'd run into that net, and it would collapse. We caught every one."

Chapter 11

During decades of travel across the southwest, Lange met many memorable people. One of these was the late J.R. Edwards of Thalia, a cowboy of the old sort known for both his skill and his pure toughness. Edwards rode in the helicopter with Lange many times, and they became friends. "He liked me. He was as tough as anyone. I don't know of anyone quite that rough, at least of that vintage."

In addition to his skill with horse and cow, Edwards was known to fight and known to be good at it. Boots O'Neal once told Lange a story about Edwards. A crew of ranch cowboys was out with the wagon, including O'Neal and Edwards. The cowboys had been pitching their dirty plates and utensils in a washtub, and not gently.

Ranch cooks are known to be surly, and this one was evidently no exception. He got tired of the noise and the mess and told the cowboys he would whip the next one who did it.

O'Neal was sitting next to Edwards, who nudged him and said, "Watch this." Edwards roughly pitched his plate into the tub, and the cook came after him. The two fought for a while, and then Edwards picked up a shovel. "That old cook grabbed a twelve-gauge shotgun and said, 'You take one more step and I'm gonna blow your head off.'" Edwards, according to the story, calmly set down the shovel, nonchalantly walked off and began catching horses.

J.R. Edwards

Lange worked for years for the late Allen Askins of Dryden, who was known to be both lively and loud. Lange stayed with Askins many nights. They played dominoes while Askins happily yelled at everyone.

Askins ranched all the way down to the Rio Grande. "He loved life. I gathered a lot of cattle for him off the river. Some of them were his, and some of them were from across the river."

It was common practice for cattlemen on either side of the Rio Grande to occasionally gather and sell the cattle that had crossed from the other side. "The

Mexican cattle would drift onto our side, and ours would drift onto their side. It was kind of a mix-up down there."

Lange never crossed the Rio Grande in his helicopter, but he worked right along it. One day he saw a jeep driving fast south of the river, and soon the Border Patrol drove up and asked if he had been flying over the border. Someone in Mexico had evidently accused him of flying south of the river.

Cattle on either side of the Rio Grande knew to flee for the river when anyone tried to gather them. They would swim across to avoid pursuit, whether it was from horsemen or a helicopter. Swimming the river was such a common thing for those cattle that the calves knew to swim upriver from their mothers, so the current pushed them into the cow rather than away from her. "They had done it enough that they knew what to do."

Another memorable character was Shelby Brooks, who owned a big West Texas ranch. "He was in his nineties when I met him. He was one of those old mean cowboys. He was tough and mean."

Lange was working for Armstrong Cattle Company, and he stayed on the ranch. One night someone invited Shelby Brooks over. "It was night, and we had a lantern because there was no electricity there." All the cowboys were sitting outside telling stories. Lange, tired from a long day, reclined on the sidewalk and listened.

Brooks told a story from when he was seventeen years old, which would have been about the 1910s, in far West Texas. Political and racial tensions were high there at the time. "That was back in the Pancho Villa days, and there were bandits coming over all the time." Brooks told the cowboys he was in a small militia of sorts.

The horseback militia was west of Van Horn, Brooks said, when they came upon a group of Mexican horsemen. "His voice got real high. He said, 'We killed them all and took their saddles.'"

Not long after that story was told, Cole Armstrong helped Brooks to his pickup so the old man could go home. When Armstrong returned, he spotted a rattlesnake next to Lange, who was still lying on the sidewalk. "I had been laying there next to him all night."

In the early 1980s Lange was occasionally hired by Lon Davis to gather the Cottonwood Pasture down in Palo Duro Canyon. "We gathered those cattle into a trap, and then we had to drive them up this road because they couldn't get trucks down in there. It was straight up."

When the cattle works were done, the owner held a big party down in the canyon. During the festivities, an unfamiliar old cowboy walked up and began talking to Lange. The friendly cowboy told Lange when he was young they camped in that very spot, but every few days they had to move their camp.

The conversation went on, and Lange asked why they had to move camp so often. The old cowboy told them they butchered a steer every few days, and they had to move away from the gut pile because of the smell.

Lange enjoyed the conversation but never knew who the man was until later, when he told Boots O'Neal about it. O'Neal told him the man had been Tom Blasingame, the legendary JA Ranch cowboy who famously stepped off his horse, lay down on the ground and died.

"Gosh, I wish I would have known who he was then. Blasingame is still a legend, how he got off his horse, crossed his arms and died."

Chapter 12

Despite all his hours in the air, Lange only had a few minor crashes, and they all occurred in his own aircraft, which was unfortunate since he was responsible for the associated costs. "I never crashed one in the military. I never crashed one of theirs. It was always mine."

He crashed his first Robinson R22 near Balmorhea. Those early Robinsons were not as powerful, at only 150 horsepower, which was not quite enough in certain situations. That was an adjustment for Lange, who was used to Hueys and even his own Bell. "I had never flown a helicopter that didn't have enough power."

A West Texas storm was coming in that day, rapidly changing weather conditions. Lange was carrying a passenger, which was quite a bit of weight for the small Robinson. Lange got the small aircraft off the ground a few feet, but it just did not have the necessary power to combat the wind. The helicopter turned on its side and fell to the ground. Fortunately, neither Lange nor his passenger were hurt. The man even remarked that he did not even spill his beer. "That was the first one I crashed."

Years later, he was hunting predators near Albany. He had been noticing the helicopter, an R22, was not performing as it should, but he could not figure out why. The change was gradual and seemed minor, but it was noticeable. "That helicopter was flying funny that day. Then, all of a sudden, we hit the ground."

The skids took the brunt of the impact, which is what they are designed to do. It turned out that the gunner had been bumping a fuel control knob every time he fired his gun, slowly turning off the gas. "He starved my engine."

Robinson Helicopters adjusted the design of that knob on all their helicopters because of the episode.

In November of 1984, Lange was flying on the Longfellow Ranch, south of Fort Stockton. They stopped the works before it was done, with plans for Lange to return soon to finish. For convenience, he left his helicopter there rather than haul it home and then back again. He had other helicopters in the hangar he could fly.

While he was gone, some cattle got out and he needed to go back quickly. He and J.Ann flew down in their Cessna 182, and they landed on the dirt strip at Eber Headquarters there on the Longfellow.

He was soon done gathering the cattle, and he and J.Ann prepared to head back to San Angelo in their Cessna. Lange taxied to the end of the dirt strip, revved the engine and was soon committed.

A Cessna 182 is a fairly powerful four-seater prop plane. It should not have had any trouble taking off. But it did. Lange fought the controls, trying to gain altitude. The Cessna rose perhaps ten feet, then crashed to the ground in the brush beyond the airstrip, almost hitting a windmill.

"The dadgum thing wouldn't come out of there. It made it a few feet, and I thought it would go on. But it would not. I crashed at the end of the runway."

The Cessna crashed nose first into the dirt, crumpling the plane. Lange and J.Ann were both wearing seatbelts, but the plane was only equipped with lap belts. They both hit the dashboard.

J.Ann was knocked unconscious. Lange carried her to a vehicle, then drove her to the hospital in Fort Stockton, where they were both admitted. J.Ann had suffered a concussion, a broken foot and needed many stitches. Lange had two black eyes but was otherwise okay.

The Cessna was totaled. One door was torn off, both wings had collapsed, and the engine was shoved almost into the cabin on J.Ann's side.

Later, Lange was talking to one of his customers, a man named Charlie Taylor, who lived near Pecos. Taylor owned an airplane and had a pilot to fly him around in it. He did not even know Lange had crashed a plane on the Longfellow Ranch, but during the course of the conversation he mentioned that he would never fly into Eber Headquarters again, not after having done it just once.

"Then I told him I had busted an aircraft in there, but he didn't even know about it before." Taylor said the same thing had almost happened to him, though in a Cessna 210.

"It's in a canyon. There's wind that comes down right there, and it catches you. I was overconfident as a pilot then, but there is something going on down there."

Because of the crash, Lange's daughter, Marsha, later did a science fair project on detecting windshear. It was so well received that she advanced to the International Science Fair and was later invited to Russia to study with cosmonauts through the People to People Youth Science Exchange.

The effects of the concussion J.Ann suffered in the plane crash ended her own piloting days. She had received her fixed wing license in 1981, and for Christmas that year Lange bought her a Cessna 182 Skylane. For many years she had flown Cessnas, often transporting various cattle buyers around the country to look at stock.

Aubrey Lange always enjoyed the helicopter business,

and it was good to him and his family financially. He lamented the fact that he was gone so much when his children were growing up, sometimes a week or more at a time.

J.Ann, Aubrey, Kyle, Marsha

"I never really got to see my kids grow up. I missed a lot of the stuff. I spent too much time doing it."

He and J.Ann bought a home and acreage on Spring Creek outside Mertzon in 1984. The scenic property sloped back toward the creek, which was lined with pecan trees and even had two waterfalls. Before they owned the property, George Strait played an outdoor concert there. Lange built a helicopter hangar on a portion of the concrete slab where Strait once played.

Over the years they purchased more land in the

vicinity, including a hunting ranch in Irion County. On this they built a lodge and a high fence, then stocked it with exotics.

Some of their properties came with mineral rights, and back in 1992 an oilfield drilling rig set up and went to work. The rig struck oil, which was an exciting time. Unfortunately, production tapered and the well brought more hope than actual income.

In addition to the exotic hunts, Lange and Kyle raised nubian ibex, which they sold live. The ibex were pretty to look at but destructive to property, which aggravated Lange considerably when they tore up his yard fence. They were also difficult to capture. Animals they sold were either trapped or shot with a tranquilizer gun. "That's the trouble. You've got to tranquilize every damn one of them."

The ibex business was profitable, though. Big males brought many thousands of dollars. "I paid for this place with them."

In 2020 Lange and J.Ann bought a bed and breakfast in Fredericksburg with their daughter Marsha, which was successful as a business but also as a real estate investment due to the significant appreciation in the area.

Kyle Lange, a skilled pilot himself, continued to grow Lange Helicopters. In 2024, the business owned ten helicopters. There was enough work to hire additional pilots for certain jobs.

J.Ann Lange

Most years Aubrey Lange logged approximately eight hundred hours, but in his busiest year he flew twelve hundred. “That’s a lot of flying.” He kept track of his hours, and he has logged a total of over 32,000. Those were mostly while he was working, as he rarely logged anything when he was not on the clock. “Anytime I didn’t get paid, I usually didn’t keep up with it.”

In 2024, when Lange sat in his kitchen and told his story, he was 81 years old. He was still flying, although he had slowed considerably and was only taking a few jobs, mostly cattle work and some deer surveys.

“Now, I guess I’m pretty well partially retired.”

Chapter 13

The following story was published by *Livestock Weekly* on November 10, 2016. Printed with permission from *Livestock Weekly*.

Texas Chopper Pilot Spent Three Weeks Gathering Alaskan Cattle

By: John Bradshaw

SAN ANGELO — When Aubrey Lange of Lange Helicopters was contacted and offered the job of gathering cattle from the air in Alaska, he didn't hesitate. He spent three weeks on Umnak Island, and it was just as much an adventure as it was work.

Bering Pacific Ranches operates on Umnak Island, one of the Aleutian Islands located southwest of Alaska. The Bering Sea lies to the north and the Pacific Ocean to the south.

Umnak Island measures roughly 16 miles wide by 70 miles in length. The terrain varies greatly, from meadows and rolling hills to steep, mountainous country and blue cinder beaches. The wind is merciless.

There are several thousand head of cattle on the island.

The vast majority are Herefords, but there are a few painted cattle. These are colored like Longhorns but bigger in body and shorter of horn. Lange was told these were the remnants of Russian cattle brought in generations ago.

The island has been so difficult to gather for years that the herd was approximately 50 percent adult bulls.

There is a small slaughterhouse on the north end of the island, and the plan this year was to gather as many cattle as possible and begin packing bulls. Lange was told there was a contract to slaughter 1400 bulls.

Live cattle can be shipped off the island, but not easily. There is no deep-water harbor, so big ships cannot make port. The only way to ship live cattle is to load them on an old military landing craft, 50-60 head at a time, and move them to a large ship.

Just getting to Umnak Island is difficult. Lange flew commercial from San Angelo to Dallas to Seattle to Anchorage to Dutch Harbor, where he boarded a helicopter for Umnak.

He was met by Josh Stamm, who lives on Umnak Island and flies for Bering Pacific Ranches. In past years the ranch was flown by two helicopters, one operated by Stamm and the other by fresh helicopter flight school graduates.

“This is not a right-out-of-flight-school deal,” Lange

said. "I've got a lot of hours, but my gosh, it's white-knuckle flying."

Many helicopters have crashed gathering the island due to the weather and the wind, and at least two pilots have been killed. Stamm pointed out one of the crash sites to Lange.

"When we came through there I could see the rotor blades stuck in the sand," he said.

The ranch furnished Lange a Robinson R22 helicopter, which he was accustomed to flying.

"It was ideal," Lange said. "You're right at sea level."

The ranch headquarters, pens and slaughterhouse are located on the north end of the island, so the pilots began on the south end, with the plan of throwing cattle together and making a big drive north.

Lange stayed at the village of Nikolski, an old Aleut

settlement, for the first half of his stay, before moving to the headquarters as the drive went north.

The first day of flying Lange and Stamm began pushing small groups of cattle together and drifting them north. That was a productive day, and they gathered 800-900 head and made 15 miles.

They never made 15 miles in a day again, and often it was as little as two. The pilots had to range farther out to pick up cattle, but the terrain was the main problem.

"There were obstacles everywhere you went," Lange said.

Streams came off the mountains that could only be crossed at certain areas because they were both deep and boggy. The first 50 head would tear up a nice crossing, and then the next thousand or so would struggle through it.

"It would take us an hour to get across one of those streams," he said.

The mountains were impassable in many areas. The beach was easy to travel for the most part, but in many areas rocky points jutted out into the water and couldn't be crossed. Then the cattle had to be driven back into the mountains and around, zigzagging through the terrain. It was slow driving.

"It would have been great if we could have stayed on

the beach, but you couldn't," he said. "Those rocks were really jagged, and you couldn't get them around."

There were spots where the cattle had to be funneled through small openings or trails maybe four feet wide, and the pilots had to slowly push through 1500 or so head.

Several steep passes were so severe that it was difficult to push the cattle down them. The cattle would occasionally slide down the hill, and Stamm told Lange that in years past there had been cattle slide down the mountain and knock down 20 more.

Late each afternoon Lange and Stamm tried to leave the cattle in an area where it wouldn't be easy for them to drift back south, but there were always cattle that turned around and headed back for their home range.

"If you didn't get back to them by daylight, they'd just filter away," Lange said. "And a lot of times the weather would shut us down until noon."

The cattle didn't drive too well, either. Most cattle know where there is a pen or water and will head that way with some encouragement. The Alaskan cattle never had to leave their small home areas and weren't used to going to a specific point.

The cattle never strung out and made a pretty herd like everyone is accustomed to seeing. These cattle wouldn't stay together well, particularly the cattle just added to the drive.

"The farther we got from their range, the more they wanted to stay together," Lange said. "That's generally true of all cattle."

Flying into Dutch Harbor

Sightseeing on Umnak Island

The large number of bulls was a constant problem. The bulls were always fighting, and it got really serious every time a cow came in heat. And cows came in heat often.

Every time a cow came in season, 10 or more bulls would go after her. The pilots would hover low and try to push the bulls away. Often they would ram the bulls with the helicopter skids.

"We'd get down there and bang on them," Lange said. "I'd bounce on their backs."

Stamm carried a pistol loaded with rat shot that he used to drive away the bulls. It got so bad that if a cow had a calf that appeared to be three to four weeks old,

Lange and Stamm assumed the cow would be coming in heat soon. When possible they'd just sort the pair and leave them behind.

"There was no sense driving that calf 40 miles anyway, because they weren't going to mark them," he said. "There were no steers on the island."

In the past the ranch had tried to only gather the bulls, but the plan didn't work. That is why the cows and calves were gathered even though nothing would be done to them.

Still, the pilots left many cattle behind because they found the animals in areas where gathering them would either be too slow or just impossible. Pockets of cattle were found in meadows surrounded by sheer walls. The cattle had feed and water and never left their valley.

"They had always been there and had kind of their own strain of cattle back in there," Lange said.

In places cattle had gone around points on the beach, and the tide came in behind them and closed them in.

Lange is used to gathering in the lower U.S., where the goal is to gather every single one. On Umnak the goal was to pick the battles. If a herd of 50 cattle were in a difficult spot, they were left alone so the drive could continue.

"We left a lot of cattle, but we had more cattle than they could handle," he said. "I would love to have gone through and cleaned it, but I don't know what for."

The painted Russian cattle were aggressive, so much so that one little black and white bull got so mad he tried to attack the helicopters.

"They were crazy aggressive," Lange said.

Most of the island is too boggy for horses, so they were never used. The cows made tracks six inches deep in the mud.

"It's a horse leg-breaking country, unless you stayed on the hard ground or on the beach."

When the drive hit the beach a man walked along on foot behind the cattle. This man was required by the ranch to carry a rifle because of the Russian bulls.

Stamm told Lange of the time he had the job of following the cattle, and he didn't take a gun. A painted bull attacked him, and Stamm finally fled into the ocean. The water was up to Stamm's neck before the bull quit fighting.

The helicopters could be refueled at either end of the island, but that put the gas far away when the helicopters were working the center of the island. The aircraft could hold three hours' worth of fuel, and Stamm and Lange each carried 10 more gallons in cans.

The gas gauge in Lange's helicopter didn't work, so it didn't take him long to figure out the machine's fuel consumption. The aircraft had a low fuel light, but Lange said those vary in accuracy from 30 seconds to two minutes.

"You don't want to find out just how long it will run after that light comes on," he said. "That's a 10-cent light."

The fuel was averaging about $15 per gallon by the time it reached Umnak Island, with all the shipping. The fuel came in on a freighter and was transferred to shore by landing craft.

Each helicopter burned 10 gallons per hour, and they were in the air eight hours most days. That puts the fuel bill at $2400 per day.

Fog was a constant concern, and it sometimes rolled in quickly. One day the fog came in when they were working on top of a mountain, trying to drive the last few cattle over the rim. The pilots stayed close enough to the ground that they could see it, but they couldn't see each other.

"I finally told Stamm, 'One of us needs to get out of here, because I can't even see where you're at,'" Lange said.

Lange eased down the mountain and found the beach, where he shut down his machine and waited for the fog to lift.

When they went for fuel, they allowed 30 minutes to fly 30 miles, because the last five miles were often in fog. There were areas near the village that were commonly foggy.

"Then you'd have to hover the last five miles following a four-wheeler trail," Lange said. "You'd just stay in contact with the ground and go like you were driving."

Robinson R22s are not meant to be flown in wind higher than 30 miles per hour, but the pilots regularly flew them in winds up to 50.

One day Lange was headed back to the cattle after refueling when the wind picked up to the point that he couldn't fly into it. He landed and stepped out to find the wind so strong he couldn't stand up in it.

"I couldn't see, because it was foggy, so I decided that was going to kill me," Lange said. "So I went back to my fueling place and waited a little while."

He believes those brief systems are what had caused so many helicopter crashes on the island in years past. The winds were at times strong enough to blow down a helicopter.

Stamm taught Lange to look at the ocean before flying

around cliffs and points, because there were places where the wind was strong enough that it pushed the water away from the island, causing waves.

“You could see where it was pushing it out, and you could be aware as you went by there because it would really be blowing,” Lange said. “It could blow you down 50 feet right quick.”

The weather wasn’t always bad, fortunately. Some days were sunny and pretty with no wind.

“You could have one really pretty day, but then you’d pay for it for two days,” Lange said.

The pilots also had to keep an eye on the eagles when they were working near the cliffs. Lange said the eagles, both bald and golden, had a habit of sitting on their perches until the helicopter was almost under them before falling off into a dive.

“They would wait until you got just right, and then they’d fall off that cliff in front of you,” Lange said. “Those silly things.”

Driftwood covered the beaches, much of it from broken docks and piers. Lange’s biggest disappointment of the entire trip was the amount of trash that had washed up on the beaches.

“It was all commercial fishing trash — buoys and nets,” Lange said. “I bet you can’t walk 10 steps without finding something."

There was some time for sightseeing, mostly as the helicopters were scouting the next day's work. Stamm served as a tour guide of sorts, showing Lange old Aleut villages, hot springs, waterfalls, volcanoes, and more. They occasionally landed and hiked for a few minutes.

"You could look at all these little villages next to the salmon streams," Lange said. "There's no telling how far those go back."

They saw reindeer, caribou and arctic fox. Caribou was on the menu, and Lange thought it was delicious.

He was originally scheduled to stay for two weeks, but Lange didn't feel right leaving Stamm with it all at that point, so he stayed another week. They were able to push the cattle up the beach and past a rocky point at low tide.

When the tide came in, the cattle couldn't go back. At the next low tide a fence was built across the beach. Lange estimates there were at least 2000 head in the herd when he left.

The terrain was easier from then on, but the work still required two helicopters. Cody Sedden, another pilot for Lange Helicopters, arrived as Lange was leaving.

"I saw him at Dutch Harbor and told him to watch

himself," Lange said.

Sedden stayed for two more weeks. When he left Umnak Island the cattle were not in the pen but were close and in an area where Stamm could handle them alone.

Lange has already been invited back for next year's gather, and he said he will go.

www.ingramcontent.com/pod-product-compliance
Lightning Source LLC
LaVergne TN
LVHW010902110826
845149LV00005B/1441

* 9 7 9 8 9 9 3 9 6 7 5 2 3 *